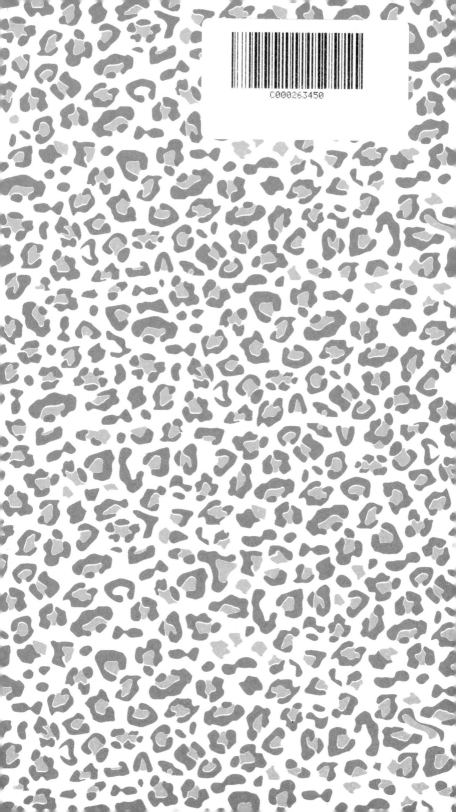

You Are
the Best
Thing Since
Sliced Bread

You Are the Best Thing Since Sliced Bread

SAMANTHA RENKE

1 3 5 7 9 10 8 6 4 2

Ebury Spotlight, an imprint of Ebury Publishing
20 Vauxhall Bridge Road
London SW1V 2SA

Ebury Spotlight is part of the Penguin Random House
group of companies whose addresses can be found at
global.penguinrandomhouse.com

Penguin
Random House
UK

First published by Ebury Spotlight in 2022

www.penguin.co.uk

A CIP catalogue record for this book is available from
the British Library

ISBN 9781529149289

Typeset in 11.65/17.65pt Adobe Garamond
by Jouve (UK), Milton Keynes
Printed and bound in Great Britain by Clays Ltd, Elcograf S.p.A.

The authorised representative in the EEA is Penguin Random House
Ireland, Morrison Chambers, 32 Nassau Street, Dublin D02 YH68

MIX
Paper from
responsible sources
FSC
www.fsc.org   FSC® C018179

Penguin Random House is committed to a
sustainable future for our business, our readers
and our planet. This book is made from Forest
Stewardship Council® certified paper.

To Carl Thomas Renke, 1957–1996
Life is short, so live it.

Contents

'The hardest thing in this world is to live in it. Be brave, live!'

Buffy the Vampire Slayer

Introduction

Hiya.

Thanks for picking up this book. It's very nice to meet you. I'm Sam. I'm 36 and I live in London with my two cats. I'm cheeky and lovable and unlovable. I love pasta, coffee, fashion, interior design, pottering around, travelling, being the centre of attention and making people laugh. I like being able to turn an awkward situation into something hilarious. I'm an overthinker and impulsive at times. I'm uninhibited and sometimes my mouth works faster than my brain.

And . . . I've written a book! But you already know that because you're reading it.

Before we go any further, the one thing I want you to know is that *you* are the best thing since sliced bread. And you know what, over the years I've learned that I am too!

I guess that's what this book is about. It's about championing ourselves. Being our own cheerleaders. I'm a great fan of the Mexican artist and thinker Frida

Kahlo and have always been struck by what I believed to be her line: 'I am my own muse.' That's what I aspire to be, and I hope this book might inspire you to become your own muse too. I later learned this has been misattributed to her and it was in fact written by artist Oroma Elewa, another strong woman. We really can't have too many in our lives.

Life can be tough. It throws us all sorts of opportunities and challenges. Sometimes it's amazing. Sometimes it's shit. Whatever it is, it's life and we're lucky to be living it.

You might think my life is very different to yours. If you know anything about me at all, you'll already know I have a disability. I was born with a rare genetic condition called osteogenesis imperfecta, which is more commonly known as brittle bone disease.

People look at me and instantly see I look different. I haven't had an accident that has left me disabled. I don't look the same as everyone else except that I happen to be in a wheelchair. I physically look different. My bones are curved. I'm just over three feet tall. So far, I've broken my bones 200 times. I've got scars. I've got features that are inherently associated with brittle bones. I look different and it's why people often stare at me.

They feel they are so far removed from me. They perhaps feel they won't be able to connect with me in any way as I look so different. But most of the hurdles I face don't come from my disability; rather, they come from things we all experience. Most of my problems stem from men and money, but more on that later.

My life has been affected by all the things non-disabled people face, including loss. My father died when I was just nine and it came totally out of the blue. He died of a brain haemorrhage, which no one could have predicted, and my life changed overnight. He was only 38 and his death left a huge hole in our family.

Despite this loss, though, I love my life. It can be exhausting, uplifting, wonderful, terrible, beautiful, ugly, amazing, depressing and myriad other things. In fact, it's pretty much like life without a disability. Sometimes it's awesome, other times not so much. It's rather like cats. Sometimes they're adorable and beguiling and at other times they're super hard work.

I want this book to do many things. I want it to tell my story. If you're disabled, I hope some of the things I say about disability will resonate with you. If you're not disabled, I hope you might learn something about disability and perhaps come to see it differently.

Most of all, though, I want to connect with you on a basic, human level and to talk about feelings and the lessons I have learned through my life.

I guess the biggest thing I want to say is that whatever you're thinking or feeling, it is valid. It's not stupid. It's normal. And, on that note, I want you to forget what you think 'normal' is. There's no such thing. I hope you'll learn a little about disability and appreciate it can be a beautiful thing. It's part of my identity and I want to share it.

Non-disabled people often spend their lives surrounded by messages that disability is all doom and gloom. It's not. Sometimes it gives you real insight. Sometimes it makes life richer.

I've been blessed with the ability to communicate, to make people laugh and smile and connect. That's been my biggest gift. Being able to share my experiences has helped some feel they're not alone and I want to broaden that reach with this book and to reiterate that life – in all its messy uncertainty – is a beautiful thing.

I genuinely love being alive, and I want to pass that on. Living is such an amazing thing, irrespective of who we are. It's a one-in-a-billion chance that we managed to get here. We are unique and that's beautiful. I think we need to reflect on that a little bit more and appreciate the beauty of who we are, irrespective of what we look like.

From my earliest age I was written off as someone who wouldn't achieve anything. Then I made the decision that I was not going to live for other people. I was going to live for myself. I said yes to things and my life changed. I feel very lucky, and I want to share my story.

Writing a book is bloody hard work. It's not the actual writing that's torturous, but more deciding what to put in and what to leave out. So, I haven't tried to structure this book in a linear fashion. Instead, I've picked certain episodes in my life and reflected on what they have taught me. I hope you'll find the lessons I've learned as useful as I have.

I also want to be clear that when I'm talking about disability, I'm relaying my own experience of it. Everyone is different and even those with the same condition can experience it in very different ways. I've tried to be honest (perhaps oversharing on occasion) because I felt it was important to be straight up.

So, thank you for picking up my book and sharing my journey. I hope you find things you can take from it and apply to your own life. After all, I always think that if I'm thinking or feeling something, then sure as hell other people are too. And we're better off together. We are, after all, the very best thing since sliced bread . . .

1

A Life Worth Living – and a Fabulous One at That!

I knew this day would come. Writing a book, I mean. It might sound strange, but I was sure from a young age I would make a positive impact on this world and people would one day know my name. I don't mean that in an egotistical way – I don't plan to change my name to 'The Renke' anytime soon. More that I knew my purpose. Tall dreams for a little person.

There's a thing I've always done whenever I desperately want to hold on to a memory. A favourite birthday, perhaps, or a special Christmas. Lying under a tree in the south of France, with the sun's rays cascading through the leaves, a gentle breeze moving them from side to side and allowing the light to bounce across my face. So beautiful, hypnotic and fleeting. A postcard moment in time I must capture forever.

I simply say to myself, over and over, that I will remember this moment. I will remember this moment while I take in every detail, as though etching it into my consciousness. I am completely present. Grateful and full of hope in that moment.

If I do this, the memory stays with me, clear as day. It's almost as though I knew it to be of importance and that I would want to dip back into it at some point in the future. It is why I can categorically say I knew I'd be writing a book and sharing my story one day. In my mind's eye, I am seven or eight and sitting on my golden Labrador Tessa's mat in the back living room of our family home. It hasn't been washed in a while and I can smell the faint wet dog aroma and feel the layer of grease and muck and the rubbery texture under my palm. None of this matters as I love to have after-school cuddles with my best friend.

It is such a bright day, and I am squinting from the sun coming in through the patio doors. Then, all of a sudden, a wave of excitement rushes through my body. I'm not sure what has prompted it – an overheard conversation, maybe, or a programme on TV – but in that moment I see my destiny. I know, I just know, that I am special, a game-changer, a force for good, and that, one day, people will know who I am.

Suddenly I have an innate sense of worth and determination. 'I'm going to be somebody,' I say to myself, giddy at the prospect, smiling. 'Remember this moment, Samantha, remember this moment.'

Before we really get into the inner workings of my mind and you get to learn an awful lot about me – the good, the bad and the fabulous; things I've never shared with anyone, even my nearest and dearest – there are a few vital pieces of information you need because, let's face it, no one really likes a blind date.

First, and most importantly, I am a huge *Buffy the Vampire Slayer* fan. Fact! Yep, you heard it right, I'm a *Buffy* über-fan. But just to clarify – and this is very important – I'm not referring to the kitsch 1992 Kristy Swanson dark comedy; sure, it had its moments and Luke Perry was kind of hot, but, no, I'm talking about the hit series from 1997 starring my queen, Sarah Michelle Gellar. That show got me through high school and even now, as an adult, I can be having the worst day and be feeling pretty deflated and all I need to do is pop on an episode of *Buffy* and I instantly feel an over-whelming sense of calm. It is my version of a baby's pacifier. I simply feel safe, as if I'm wrapped in a teddy-bear duvet. It is the sense of familiarity. I know what I'm getting when I watch it.

Buffy has also become a part of my identity. Anyone who knows me well knows I'm huge fan and the show, like a signature perfume, has been associated with me since I was a teenager. I'm almost proud to have a passion in my life, even if it is just a teen series. It's a part of me and one of the reasons I wanted to get into acting. But I'm getting ahead of myself.

Secondly, although I sound unmistakably northern and am a proud Lancashire lass who often forgets to use the word 'the' (as in 'put it on table'), I was born in Germany. My last name, Renke, is Germanic-sounding but, while my mother is German, my surname comes from my British father. From the scraps of information I've been able to piece together, my grandfather, George, came from Lithuania and, during the Second World War, he escaped from whatever nightmare he found himself in and ended up in America. As a foreigner and a non-English-speaking fella, he decided that, to blend in with Western civilisation, he would shorten his tough-to-pronounce surname to Renke. None of our family knows what his original name was and I hate to burst your bubble, Granddad, but Renke still sticks out like a sore thumb. After all, the name Renke is hardly Smith or Wilson, is it?

It's a strange thing to have a unique last name and I should point out early on that it is pronounced with a silent 'e', although most of the teenage boys I went to school with would only interact with me if they called me Renkeeeeeeee. Never Samantha or Sam. Simply Renkeeeeeeee. My point here is to be proud of your identity even if people cannot for the love of cheese pronounce your surname correctly. You may have an unusual name, or hair that goes wild in the rain. You may be super tall or have an unusual accent. You may be brilliant at spelling or terrible at maths. But it's all these elements that make up what is essentially you. Sure, you can change things if you want to, but embracing the quirky, unusual and uniquely *you* bits of you is surely a better way to go.

Another piece of information about me that I feel the need to share – perhaps unwisely – is that my pubic hair grows straight, not curly. And when I say straight, I mean it looks like I've taken a pair of GHDs to my pubis. This is, of course, an absolute overshare, but I've never found the right time or place to bring it up in conversation and I'm dying to ask if this is something other women experience? So, please, if you too have salon-quality, coiffured straight pubic hair, seek me out on social media and DM me. I'd like to take comfort in the fact that I'm not the only straight pubis'd person out there.

Continuing in confessional mode, another thing I'd like to admit is that I'm also really bad at spelling. I can still remember cheating in my primary school spelling tests. Thinking I was sly as feck, I would lift the lid on my wooden school table, balance it on my head, the weight pushing into my crown, and rummage around pretending to find my rubber when really I was looking at my pre-written cheat sheet.

To this day, I totally pretend to know words I have no clue about – like, all the time. So often I've looked at Wikipedia on my phone, under a table, just so I can understand what's going on during a meeting. Take the word 'nuanced'. I'm still not clear how to use it or what it means, but I see and hear it everywhere. I've looked it up a bunch of times, but somehow it just won't stick. It's like 'effected' and 'affected'. Who really knows? So

I've learned to simply throw words into a sentence and hope for the best. It's all about how confidently you deliver them. It totally throws people off and they think you know what you are doing.

Writing this book, then, has been pretty darn hard. Harder than I expected. I didn't think it would be a walk in the park, but, jeez, the sleepless nights, the imposter syndrome and the wishing I'd listened more to my wonderful English teacher, Mrs Gardner, when she told me to stop repeating words and shorten my sentences. Show don't tell.

What I'm trying to say is don't let the small things hold you back. If you want to write a book, but are terrible at spelling, who cares? Worry about that bit later. Plus, there are all sorts of things – from autocorrect to editors – that are there to help. If you have something you want to share with the world, then share it!

Another fun fact and an absolute need-to-know about me is that I adore fashion and can visualise each and every garment in my wardrobe, under my bed, stuffed in my airing cupboard, or in vacuum-packed bags. I can bring them all together – the handbags and shoes, the whole shebang – and arrange them in my mind like some computer software programme or those fuzzy felt dollies you dress up to create a flawless ensemble. I may not have many raw talents but this, folks, is a skill and one I thought everyone possessed until people started to come to me for fashion advice.

Even bigger than my love of fashion is my love of interior design. It's taken over my little flat in Shoreditch, East London. I've learned that I just like pretty things. Pretty, not expensive. Like my *Buffy* passion, having a home that reflects my personality and style brings me calm. It's a tricky one to explain if you aren't into interiors, but you know that little flutter you get when it's Christmas and you wake up on a rainy and miserable-AF day, then you switch on your twinkle lights and somehow the harshness from the bitter cold outside isn't so harsh any more? Well, that's the feeling I get every time I come home. Calm. Independence. My little sanctuary.

Lastly – and possibly most importantly – I am a devoted and rather eccentric Sphynx cat mother. I always thought I was a dog person, but here I am with two Sphynx cats. Yep, Sphynx cats. My baby girl, Lola, is literally my BFF and my drinking partner because, you know what they say, you aren't drinking alone if the cats are at home. Then there is Bruno, who is named after my German 'Opa', aka granddad, who is dead and therefore can no longer get annoyed that I named my cat, who looks like a scrotum, after him.

For those unfamiliar with the breed, just think back to that *Friends* episode – 'The One with the Ball' – in which Rachel buys a pink, furless fur baby and carries it on a velvet pillow. The one in which Joey sees the furless nugget and yells: 'THAT IS NOT A CAT!'

There are like a gazillion memes out there about how these cats resemble a plucked chicken or a ball sack, or that they are the devil's spawn. The poor sods really do get a hard time. They are undoubtably the Marmite of the cat world. People either love them or hate them with a fiery passion. So why on earth would I opt for an alien-looking cat as my pet instead of a fluffy, soft-on-the-eye breed like a Persian? Well, put simply, I see myself in them. No, I don't resemble a wrinkled scrotum and I am not the product of incest. Instead, like me, Sphynx cats are a genetic mutation. They're a fluke: unique, intelligent and extremely affectionate. Yet some may argue they are not supposed to exist – the Sphinxes we know today began in 1966 in Ontario, Canada, when a short-haired cat gave birth to a bald kitten which, as icky as it sounds, was then mated back with its mother. At least, that's how the story goes. But the result is a wonderfully distinctive and special breed.

My list of things you need to know about me ends with the fact that I was born with a rare condition called osteogenesis imperfecta. Can you see where I'm going with this one? As I mentioned earlier, osteogenesis imperfecta is more commonly known as brittle bone disease, but I much prefer the term condition. I mean, 'disease' sounds like I have syphilis and warts and stuff. I can categorically say that you can't catch brittle bones from me. Perhaps the odd cold sore, but no harm will come to you from my brittle bones unless you really piss me off and I run you over in my power wheelchair.

I'm not diseased. That just sounds rooted in ableist oppression, where you'd lock disabled people away or see them as untouchable. I'm just different from your typical person or what society sees as 'normal'.

My condition is genetic, which, by definition, means it is inherited from parents or someone in your bloodline. Yet, true to form – I had to be the overachiever – I was born with a mutated version of brittle bones that doctors call type three. Neither Mama nor Papa Renke has the condition – and, no, they are not related, which, rather horrifyingly, is a question they have been asked on more than one occasion. As far as we can tell, no one else in our family has the condition. I am one of a kind and I've always sort of loved that about me.

So, without wanting to sound like a medical journal, what is osteogenesis imperfecta and how does it impact my life? Here are some fun facts.

Contrary to popular belief, eating a block of cheese each morning isn't a cure. I shit you not. You'd be surprised how many people upon hearing of my condition decide to embark on what can only be described as 'disabledsplaining' and insist that brittle bones will go away if I just eat more cheese. News flash: no amount of Babybel or Red Leicester will undo my genetic make-up or alter my genome.

I suppose I get the connection some people try to make between brittle bones and calcium intake, but I mean, come on, guys. Apart from being completely unsolicited, patronising and grossly inaccurate advice, this kind of ableist microaggression is totally infuriating to the point where I simply want to poke people in the eye with a carrot and yell, 'SHUT UP!'

Brittle bones isn't a calcium deficiency. Just like anyone else, my calcium consumption only helps to keep my bones strong as much as it would the next person. Instead, it's a collagen issue. To be more specific, a deficiency of type one collagen. Yes, collagen – that stuff some people like to pump into their lips and cheeks. We naturally produce different kinds of collagen to help our teeth, bones, skin and arteries stay strong and durable. In my case, there's a lack of it, which affects the density of my bones.

I get a lot of people asking if I will ever be cured and the odd person on the street will literally lay their hands on me and say I can be cured if I subscribe to whatever religion or fad diet they are advocating. There is no cure for brittle bones and, gosh, we really have this obsession with curing and changing people, don't we?

Let me make this crystal clear: I have never wanted to and will never want to be cured of brittle bones. Most disabled people I've met feel the same way about their condition, their chronic illness, neurodivergence and so on. Sure, we don't want to be in pain or unwell, and sometimes we do get sick of the skin we are in, but we are who we are and being made to constantly feel like we aren't good enough is draining and darn rude.

Take a moment and ask yourself how you would feel if someone continually questioned your sexuality, race, ethnicity, religious belief or gender? It wouldn't feel too great, would it? So why assume disabled people want to be cured? We'll come back to this point a little later.

A doctor once described my condition really well to me. As a visual learner, it's stuck with me. I find it useful whenever I'm trying to explain brittle bones to anyone unfamiliar with the condition. Think of bone like an Aero chocolate bar (or any chocolate bar with bubbles in it). If you cut that chocolate bar in half, you would see it has a host of tiny bubbles inside it. Bones are like that. However, the bubbles in my bones have gone that bit extra. I mean of course they have! Instead of being teeny tiny ones, they're pretty much gaping craters, which means my bone density and the stability and elasticity of my bones are pretty weak and temperamental. I've had around 200 broken bones to date, and they began in utero. Clearly, I was a disco baby and enjoyed jumping around in my mum's womb, but it meant multiple fractures even before I came into this glorious world.

When I was born, my bones – including my skull – were so fragile that during my formative months I had to be carried around on a pillow rather than cradled in my parents' arms. Again, we wonder why I turned out to be such a fierce and fabulous – if not melodramatic – diva, considering I started my life like an Egyptian princess. Cleopatra clearly had nothing on me.

Another fun fact. Even though I have had so many fractures, each and every one still hurts like a mother-fucker. 'But you must just get used to it, don't you, Sam?' people ask. No. I do not. It's just another of those annoying questions. I'm less sure of the logic behind it and, rather than wanting to poke them in the eye with a carrot, I'm inclined to say: 'Well, let's find out, shall we? Pass me that hammer over there and let's start bashing your knees repeatedly and see if you get used to it?'

I am not a violent person. I know you may be questioning that right about now, but I am a pacifist. I even cried when I once rolled over a grasshopper with my wheelchair and still feel guilty to this day. But when you're faced with the constant bombardment of insensitive and ignorant comments and incessant questions about your condition, you can sometimes want to snap, even if it is just in your head.

So, I guess it's a bloody good thing I'm writing this book, so I can get it all out in the open and set the record straight. To be clear: breaking bones, no matter how often you do it, hurts. You never get used to it. There are degrees of damage. There are little hairline fractures that can happen on a weekly basis as a result of a simple movement, such as picking up the kettle or sneezing. Then there are more serious compound or clean breaks that can ironically also happen from, well, picking up the kettle or sneezing. Or, more often than not in my case, drinking too much vodka while wearing slippery tights and falling off the toilet.

Last time this resulted in me cracking my skull and fracturing my collar bone in two places. Not my finest moment, granted, but I was having fun with one of my oldest and closest friends, Kate, up until that point, so all in all it wasn't quite as bad as it sounds. Plus, I learned a valuable life lesson in the process. Not to wear sheer slippery black tights ever again.

For those of you who've never experienced a broken bone, firstly, you lucky bastards. Bone pain is a weird pain that's uniquely specific. It's not a bruise or an ache or a sting, it's a combination of all these things. When it happens, you instantly know. Not necessarily because the pain comes straight away, but because a hit of adrenaline washes over you as if your body is preparing to go into battle: shields up, swords drawn. And it's not until moments later that the searing, flame-like heat comes coursing through your arm or your leg. It's as if someone's lit a match inside your body. As it starts, you can hear your heartbeat in your ears, pounding much louder and faster than normal.

If you are a pro like me, you'll know to keep still for as long as possible. You try to keep still because as soon as you start to move, the real pain kicks in as the free nerve endings present throughout your bones are severed and they start to realise what the fuck just happened and wake up. Ergo pain. Then gravity begins to play its part. Under normal circumstances we are extremely grateful to have gravity on our side because it keeps our bottoms from floating off into outer space, but when you have a fracture, gravity wants to pull that bone down. In particular, when you have a broken femur or a collar bone, gravity is your worst nightmare. Every single move can be excruciating, as though someone has tied a piece of string to the fracture and keeps bloody tugging on it.

The best is when you are on your way to the hospital in an ambulance. Seriously, ambulances feel like they have zero suspension. You can literally feel every single bump. I mean, the one vehicle that should glide like an eco-hybrid carrying precious cargo feels more like you're on the Wild Mouse ride at Blackpool Pleasure Beach. Every time the driver puts on those brakes it feels like someone's pushing your fracture to the ground.

Another misconception is that people with brittle bones take longer to heal. Surprisingly, we heal somewhat faster than the average Joe. Not by much – we aren't secret superhumans – and there is a logical explanation. Think back to the chocolate analogy and the bubbles and imagine some tiny Playmobile figures frantically trying to fill in those gaping holes. These miniature builders are always working on my bones because my body knows they are pretty shoddy and weak, so when I fracture, the healing process begins immediately. If you don't have brittle bones, your little builders are always on sabbatical – until, that is, the day that you might break something. All this means your body takes a little more time to get going on the healing process. The downside of having these little builders constantly in action is that we tend to sweat an awful lot. Sweaty palms were a high school nightmare for me. Our bodies are constantly working overtime, so we experience fatigue too.

I am much more than my diagnosis, yet I am so incredibly proud of my disability identity, even with all of its distinguishing complex characteristics. Truth be told, I'm sharing my condition with you because throughout my life, like many disabled people, I have been at the receiving end of countless questions about why I'm so small, why I look different and – my personal favourite – 'what's wrong with you?'

For all the negative comments I get, I am hugely positive about my disability and the opportunities I get to make a difference in the world. I do a lot of work on making things more inclusive and accessible and have so many fingers in different pies that I often describe myself as the Del Boy of the disability community. Don't get me wrong: my life isn't always easy but being grateful for all that is good and being able to see the positives makes life a hell of a lot easier, I can tell you.

Being yourself and embracing all that is uniquely you is one of the hardest, but most valuable, life lessons you can learn. Sure, we could all spend hours every day wishing we were blonder or darker, less geeky, more geeky, or a zillion other things, but it takes so much less effort and is so much more rewarding to simply learn to love ourselves as we are.

2

What Is Normal?

'In order to be irreplaceable, one must always be different.'

Coco Chanel

Words have power. They can make or break us. Build us up or tear us down. We must choose them wisely. They have the potential to define us. Their energy can linger, circling our brain like a plane ready to land. Infecting our thoughts. Totally sneaky, ready to pounce when we least expect, plunging us into absolute self-doubt and playing havoc with our self-worth.

Sticks and stones can totally break our bones but words can bloody hurt too. A 'flippant' remark. An outdated trope. An ignorant comment. A label. A micro-aggression, often described as being like death by a thousand paper cuts. That primary school teacher's frustrated remark that 'if you hit my desk with your wheelchair again, I will throw you and it out of the window', which stays with you even though they thought you were too young to remember. The school bullies' taunts: 'midget', 'Mini-Me', 'spaz'. And the biggest and most often loudest voice of all: the internal voice telling you that you aren't good enough, you don't belong. The power of words.

I know that words only have power if you believe in them. If you believe you are beautiful, ugly, a failure, a success. Yet I often wonder how you carve out your own path, negate a label, go against the grain and own a word. Give it new meaning. How do you take away the power given to it by others and make it your own? How can one person take on the world and challenge and redefine language?

Well, for starters, you are not alone. One of the main reasons I am writing this book is because I'm an over-thinker, a worrier. As a child this presented itself in night terrors, vomiting, being awake in a dream state, eyes rolled back and sobbing uncontrollably. I adopted obsessive-compulsive behaviour. I took on countless routines. Each night I'd have to tuck my dolls into their crib because if I forgot, something terrible would happen. Before my dad died, I was worried I would fracture; after my dad died, I would worry about losing my mother. The crib was really cute. It was red with gingham curtains, and it would rock. As a child I would bum shuffle as I didn't use my wheelchair at home. At night I would shuffle across the room and tuck the dolls in with the duvet my grandma had made.

I have been gifted with the power of the 'gob'. You hear me before you see me, and I love that about me. My laugh has been described as a witch's cackle (but at least I'm laughing). My neighbour in the flat above often reminds me that he can hear me singing through the floorboards (at least I'm not crying).

I'm loud and proud and, at three feet something tall, I take that as a win. In all honesty I really don't have a filter. I'm not scared to share and discuss almost every ounce of my life with anyone who is up for listening. I truly believe that most of our suffering and heartache comes from silence. I guess that's where the phrase 'to suffer in silence' originates.

We are fooled into thinking that what makes us human – our flaws, our thoughts and behaviours, our heartaches, our failures, and our abject insecurity – are things to keep hush-hush. Expressing ourselves and being unapologetically imperfect are seen as things we should be embarrassed by, and we're taught to believe that our mistakes should be mulled over alone. In isolation.

Conversely, what I've learned through my tendency to overshare and my bold voice is that we all experience the same insecurities and ruminate on the same issues. We just aren't talking about it and instead we feel alone. We suffer in silence. Too scared to ask, *Hey, are you scared, too? Did this happen to you too? Is it okay for me to feel this way? Does this make me a bad person? Should my pubic hair look like this?*

Well, I'm here to break the silence and to prove my theorem that there are a few things about me that I can guarantee are relatable. For starters, I have way too many nipple hairs. My boobs are asymmetric – so much so I went to my GP and asked for a breast augmentation. I didn't go through with it but I also didn't take my bra off during sex for many years. I prefer the company of pets to the company of people. I've judged someone on their appearance before getting to know them. I often think I am unworthy of love and will die alone and be eaten by my cats.

I'm far more materialistic than I'd like to be. I can be a selfish prick at times. I've lied in the past to get out of work or meeting with friends, saying I'm unwell but, in reality, I couldn't be bothered to shower or just didn't like the vibe. I should never have smiled and said 'yes, of course I'd love to go for drinks' before giving out my number. And when I was 11, I stole a sweet at the supermarket but felt so guilty I spat it out before I got to the checkout and had anxiety attacks every time my mum wanted to go back there.

From time to time, I still fall into the trap of silence and start to question everything. The biggest question – the one that repeatedly rears its ugly head – is: *Am I normal?* Are my low energy levels normal? Are my neurotic over-analysing tendencies normal? Is my body normal? Is it normal that I don't get aroused by pictures of men's penises? Is my rather chubby vagina normal? Is the fact that I find my own sense of humour hilarious normal? Is my longing to live in a hut and buy a goat normal?

Then I give myself a good old telling off. Samantha, who gives a fuck about being normal? You've never been normal but that's never stopped you. You've taken the word normal, redefined it and spat it back out. Give yourself a break.

The word *normal* has followed me around from day dot. It was imposed on me like a parasitic twin. It lingered like an eggy fart. It was given to me so I'd know my place in the world. Keep me from getting too big for my boots. Stop me from dreaming or having aspirations. This is normal and you, Samantha, aren't, so stay within the parameters of your label, because if you stray the world won't know what to make of you or what to do with you. Stick to your label because it's safer, less risky. Challenging it will only cause you more pain and suffering.

But I have challenged it. Seen it for what it is. A word. A word used to control, suppress and oppress. A word used to 'other' me. Attempting to define normal is society's way of saying, 'No, you can't sit with us.' A word only has power if you allow it. Well, I don't allow normal to define me. This epiphany, though, didn't come so easily. There was a time when those six letters dictated who I was.

So, let's rewind a little. To 16 January 1986, the day of my birth. That's right, I'm a Capricorn on the cusp of Aquarius. In a hospital room in Münster, a historic town in northwest Germany – known for its medical universities – defined by beautiful Gothic buildings and cobble-lined streets. My mother, Ingeborg, but known to everyone as Ina, worked as a nurse and lived in a nearby village called Altenberge. She met my father, a soldier in the British Army. Neither of them were fluent in the other's language but what did that matter? Both of them were incredibly attractive individuals. I've seen the pictures. I mean, my mum was a total Betty, and my dad had a suave, brooding thing going on. I always imagined them as a modern-day Romeo and Juliet, without the family disapproval and the rather sticky end.

My mum has told me that they'd party until the early hours of the morning at the army barracks and then she would get in her pride-and-joy orange Volkswagen Beetle and make her way to start the morning shift at the hospital, totally brushing over the fact she was probably too sleep-deprived to be driving anywhere, never mind starting her shift looking after sick people. This is normally when parents protest that it was 'different back then'.

They married on 2 May 1980, and the next year they had my older sister, Stephanie, who was born healthy with no underlying conditions. When Mum became pregnant for the second time a few years later, my family was on its way to becoming the postcard-perfect, suburban, two-point-four unit.

Medical technology, however, wasn't as sophisticated back then. Ultrasounds weren't really capable of identifying much more than a heartbeat. It came as a huge shock and surprise to everybody involved when I was born with brittle bones. A squidgy little infant with bowed legs and multiple fractures. Osteogenesis imperfecta type three.

From what I have been told, the labour went like any other and I was delivered much like any other baby. Delivering a baby as fragile as I was in a conventional way, however, was a recipe for disaster. I came into this world in pain. But bones heal and pain can be soothed. What was worse, and what lingered, was that I came into this world with a label. A label I had no part of or say in. I was given a label rooted in so much oppression, toxicity and misinformation. I was labelled as wrong. Abnormal. Deformed. Disabled.

Not long ago I met up with my dad's best friend and army pal, Andy, his brother from another mother. I wanted to talk to him about the things my father had said about me. He had two girls of similar ages to me and my sister and – all four girls being blonde – we could have been siblings. I was the baby of the bunch so my kaleidoscopic memories are triggered by old photographs of us: messy haired and half asleep; opening presents from Santa on Christmas Day; playing in the bathtub together. We wore matching purple and green shell suits, the sort that were highly flammable, and we all had the same Goofy slippers. Our hair had been cut into uniform blonde bobs complete with poker-straight fringes.

Andy stayed in the service much longer than my father and I remember us sending him care packages that typically included loo roll, soap and stick-figure drawings I did for him. Steph and I were always so excited to receive letters back from whichever base he happened to be at. We knew they were from him because they came on blue paper, and it made me feel so grown up getting my own post.

Our reunion was so magical. Although much older, Andy was still just as ruggedly handsome, with a James Bond swagger. He was family and seeing him gave me a warm feeling in my tummy like mulled wine on a winter's day. But with over 20 years to catch up on, where to start, what to ask? Of course, I wanted to know so much about the good old days, about my dad, all the juicy gossip, but I had one burning question – what did Dad do or say when I was born? I asked because my dad seemed to carry the weight of the world on his shoulders, and I knew he somehow felt guilty, as if my having brittle bones was in some way his fault. He was so terrified even to hold me. I remember one time when my mum, who was my main caregiver, was sick and in bed, flat out with flu, leaving my dad in charge of childcare duties. That evening he carried me upstairs to bed, every ounce of him trembling, so fearful he'd hurt me. But like most men he was not one to show his emotions and I have only one recollection of him ever crying. It was when my godson, Daniel, who also had brittle bones, passed away just before his first birthday. We all cried that day. Rather unusually, I was seven when I became his godmother and it was a role I took very seriously.

Andy told me that not long after my birth my dad left the hospital and visited him. 'He came round to our flat and told me that you had been born,' he said. 'But the expected look of a proud new father had been replaced by a man whose eyes were filled with tears. I initially thought the worst, that you or your mum did not survive the birth. But we sat on the couch and your dad started to tell me the extent of your birth injuries. As he spoke, the tears welled up in our eyes. I had never heard of brittle bones, so I couldn't understand how this could happen. I just imagined an innocent baby coming into the world in pain.

'I sat on the couch with your dad, and we just hugged as one father would hug another in such a situation. Your dad was my brother and my best friend, more than my own siblings. I don't know how long we sat for but eventually he had to leave to go back to the hospital to be with your mum.

'It was a couple of days before we were allowed to visit, and I remember looking down at you, wondering how this could happen. I remember the first time I was allowed to hold you, I was so scared that I could hurt you just by holding on too tight.'

I have so much sorrow and anger surrounding my birth and the weeks and months that followed. I'm angry and frustrated because nobody has the right to label, define, cast off or dismiss anybody, particularly on what should have been a joyous day. Even when the doctors had identified my condition as OI, the narratives still stayed the same. Let's just say everyone had definitely taken their Negative Nancy pills that day. *She can't; she won't; she shouldn't. I'm sorry; the poor thing; what a shame; how cruel.* Jeez, crack a smile – it's not a Greek tragedy, it's a wonderful miracle. It's the birth of a child.

I truly wish I could somehow go back and astral project my current self into that delivery room. It would probably scare the shit out of my parents, but it would definitely be worth it to simply be able to say: 'Don't worry, Mum and Dad, and certainly don't listen to them. I am living my best life.'

So, let me play devil's advocate just for a moment. Of course, everyone was blindsided by my arrival being accompanied with a complex condition such as osteogenesis imperfecta type three and, of course, the doctors and healthcare professionals had a duty of care and a legal obligation to tell my parents the facts and what, if any, treatments or support were available. These are totally important, and I'd be condemning them if they hadn't been straight with my parents. I also do not blame my dad for being completely devastated. A father's role is to protect. I can only imagine how utterly helpless he felt. A baby being born with multiple fractures, in pain and not being able to understand that pain, is heartbreaking. No loving, caring human wants suffering, especially for an innocent infant. Nevertheless, I still feel anger that the essence of hope was taken away from us all. Without hope all is lost.

It was as though my diagnosis had already defined me and I'd barely taken my first breath. No joy, no words of encouragement. Simply doom and gloom. Because life with a disability or chronic condition is still deemed by many to be a life not worth living. An inferior existence. A joyless or hopeless life. I am here to tell you all that a disabled life is a beautiful, rich and joyful life. It isn't a tragedy. An inherently bad thing. This is so fucking wrong on so many levels and such a damaging narrative. A life with a disability isn't a bad one, it is full of love, hope, joy and excitement. It isn't a death sentence or an unfortunate outcome. 'What a shame, the poor parents, she will never have a normal life.'

It used to irritate me so much when I'd hear parents-to-be say, 'I don't care if they're a boy or a girl – just as long as they're happy and healthy.' As a disabled child I used to think, *What happens if they're not healthy? Will you love them any less?* Of course not – and having a child who is neurodivergent or physically disabled doesn't automatically mean they will live an unhappy life. This way of thinking is so harmful and so ableist. It sees disability as a problem, something to be fixed or cured. This isn't about pretending such a child may not need support or additional care in place, such as operations or medication, wheelchairs, walking aids, breathing or feeding tubes. Rather, it's about acknowledging that each of us – no matter who we are – is unique and we all need help and support from others throughout our lives.

So, please stop condemning disabled children to a life you perhaps can't envision because you have subscribed to what society has told you about disability. Because you can only see the bad and not the good, because you hold success and happiness to be the most important things and you cannot begin to fathom that someone else's life is worth living even if it is a different life. Viewed through those myopic eyes, you are totally missing the bigger picture.

As I've already mentioned, most of my life's woes come not because of my condition but from two things: money worries and men. My disability only becomes an 'issue' when other people make me feel like a problem. Disability is a social construct. I become disabled not because of brittle bones, but because of social barriers, other people's attitudes and my environment.

An example. I live in a flat in London that has been adapted to improve accessibility. I have an automatic front door; one click of a button and – *voilà* – it opens, which is really handy when I come home pissed as a fart and can't find the keyhole. The windows, too, are automatic. I have a wet room instead of a bathroom with a bath, wider doors, lower light switches, and higher plug sockets so I can reach them from my wheelchair. The oven in the kitchen is lower and opens vertically not horizontally and my cooking hob is on hydraulics so it can be raised or lowered depending on who's cooking.

I've been able to put my own stamp on the flat, so it's quite bohemian. There's lots of wood and throws and my bedroom is like a French boudoir. I have a cast-iron bed and a feature wall. It's very serene. There's a huge feather lamp in the corner. My flat very much represents my character. Every room has a different story to tell. It's my sanctuary and I'm at my happiest here. I love having duvet days, eating huge bowls of pasta or peanut butter ice cream here.

I have brittle bones. And that won't go away even if you stick me on the moon. But in my adapted home I am not disabled. I am independent. I have complete autonomy over my life, and I am free to be me. As soon as I leave my front door, however, I become disabled because of myriad obstacles in my way. Poorly maintained pavements, rubbish or bicycles blocking dropped kerbs, people who talk to the person I'm with instead of to me because they assume I can't speak for myself. The fact that most London Underground stations don't have step-free access. That the bar my friends are in is in a basement with no lift. The list goes on and on. Only when the world sees me as a burden do I become frustrated and, well, a little pissed off. Then I start to believe that I'm wrong. That I am the problem.

I'm here to show you all that a life with a disability is most certainly a life worth living and I wouldn't change who I am for all the Louboutins in the world (not that I can wear them anyway – I have kids' size nine feet!).

This book is filled with a whole bunch of clichés. You know the sort; like when your gran tells you that life is too short, to seize every opportunity or you might regret it. Or when your high school teacher says that your school days are your best and youth is fleeting so enjoy it while you can. Or those smug people on the internet who look like they have it all figured out, who practise wellbeing and self-care and insist that the key to life's happiness is taking time for yourself to relax instead of running the rat race or living for other people.

If you're like me, most often you'll simply roll your eyes or offer back a vague stare while thinking, *Oh please, for heaven's sake, do shut up, you patronising, know-it all little git!* It's never easy having others impose their opinions on your life even if it comes from a loving and caring place and, sometimes, we find it hard to accept that perhaps our parents, teachers and the bendy yoga people on Instagram may actually have a point.

There is indeed a lot of truth in these little pearls of wisdom. I'm not too sure why I ever doubted these knowledge nuggets because, let's face it, they have been around for eons and if it ain't broke ... That's another cliché, perhaps, but it doesn't detract from the glaringly obvious – that living your best life, no matter who you are, doesn't have to be hard work.

The tools we have already been given – passed down from one generation to the next – have evolved through scholars, philosophers, prophets, communities and social media influencers. The hard part, however, is implementing them and believing in ourselves. So, why do we often forsake our own wellbeing and success and find simple acts of self-love so darn bloody difficult? Why can it be so hard to take time to appreciate what you have rather than dwelling on what you don't? To exist in the moment and the present, instead of living with regret? And, above all, to be grateful and unequivocally unapologetic for who you are because you are pretty darn magical? Why aren't we all moving heaven and earth to make this happen for ourselves?

On the surface these life hacks may seem easy as pie and common sense but putting them into practice is no lemon meringue. These are lessons you need to learn by yourself, not from some old relative or a YouTuber. Sure, they can point you in the right direction, but it's your life journey and you need to do things in your own time and at your own pace. Even now as I sit and write this book, I am not a complete package, and I guess I never will be. That's okay because I love learning and growing. I now enjoy being in my own head and with my own thoughts. I've learned to analyse my own behaviour. If I've snapped at someone or been frustrated, I will work out why I have felt like that. I've identified I have abandonment issues and, as I get older, I need to rely on more people for help. It has been challenging having to work with people, so I feel quite proud of myself that I'm not as reactive now. I can take a breath before I act. I've learned to take a step back.

I love how different I am now – in my thirties – compared to my 20-year-old self. I have learned to analyse a situation and if something was my fault, I have learned to apologise. I have learned to better communicate my needs and to know that I shouldn't feel like I'm a burden just because I'm asking for assistance.

Learning to identify where my feelings come from and being more mindful about my reaction has been a huge lesson for me, as has learning to ask for what I need. I think we can all help ourselves hugely by learning to take a moment to consider how we would like to react to a situation rather than just doing so instinctively in a way that might not be the most helpful to ourselves or others.

I love to look back at my triumphs – such as saying yes to being on live TV for the first time without media training – and my cringe blunders and epic Lord-what-were-you-thinking moments – like when I moved to London and put up with a very toxic friendship or doing work things for free – and see myself evolve from caterpillar to cocoon to butterfly. The caterpillar isn't any less than, or inferior to, the butterfly. Rather, the caterpillar is integral to its existence. I'm like cookie dough not yet baked and, let's face it, the best cookies are the ones that are all squidgy in the middle with a crispy crust.

The reality is you often only really understand these pearls of wisdom after some of your most heartbreaking or momentous life-changing moments. It's almost as if the universe doesn't want to give up its wonders for free. But, let's face it, even when you think you've found your happiness and your wisdom, you don't always cling on to it as perhaps you should. Life gets in the way or, as the cool kids say, 'shit happens'. One minute you think you have it all sorted – you've worked on yourself, and you are proud of the person you've become: a strong, self-assured, boss bitch – then, just like that, a new job, a new partner, ill health or a global pandemic comes crashing in and you crumble the way a sandcastle being washed away by the tide dissipates in an instant. All your time and effort is gone in one moment and, before you know it, you are consumed with the pressures of the world, you forget who you are and what you want to be and instead become obsessed with a successful YouTuber and wish you could have their life instead of yours.

Right now, I don't have a support assistant and that's one of my biggest challenges. I take it very personally when they leave because it has such a big effect on my ability to work and live. That happened during the pandemic and has led me to move in with my mum for a bit. I used to really pander to my assistants in the hope it would make them not leave, but now I have learned that nothing I can do will make a difference and I have to just trust it will all work out.

Twenty-first-century living is darn difficult, no doubt about that. We aren't being eaten by dinosaurs any more, but I feel consumed most days with a feeling of loneliness, like I'm not good enough. My heart races and I feel physically sick. I'll wake up around 4am and have an anxiety attack. Because I'm in a half-asleep state I find it difficult to practise mindfulness to reassure myself.

It's so hard to see the positives in a world that pushes negativity and unhealthy forms of competition. You won't be happy until you reach 10,000 followers (make that 20,000). Oh, wait, have you not got a blue tick? If you aren't verified, you don't actually exist and anything you say or do is rendered mute. You are only a good Samaritan if you take a selfie as you give that homeless person a Starbucks and upload it to Facebook to show the world you are caring. Otherwise karma doesn't work.

I compare myself with others on social media a lot. It's difficult for most of us not to, but no good ever comes from it. Once we accept that we're comparing how we feel inside to what others want to project into the world, it becomes a little easier to be less harsh on ourselves, but it doesn't come without practice. Oh, and don't forget that your life's worth is also not defined by which car you buy, the size of your house, your sausage dog or whether you lather yourself in this overpriced and stinky lotion. Wow, that went a little Fritz Lang *Metropolis*. No more Marxism, I promise.

Even without external factors, we humans are programmed to survive, fight or flight, not to sit back and work on our inner being, or reflect on hard times and assess the good that comes out of a bad experience. I refer to this as the toothache effect. I'm pretty sure we've all experienced toothache and I'm pretty sure that when we have, we would sell our gran simply to stop the pain. But, once the pain has gone, we forget all about it and, instead of reflecting on the joys of what health feels like, we simply pick up where we left off.

Then, of course, there is negativity bias, where we tend to focus more on the negative things in our life rather than the positive. You can have a zillion people tell you that you are beautiful, but if one nasty Twitter troll says you are ugly then that is all you can think about. You may even start to internalise that one nasty comment and come to believe it. I guess it's something to do with our lizard brain. I'm not the best person to talk psychology. I took one class in college and was humiliated on the first day.

Sitting in the classroom, it gradually became apparent to me that I'd unknowingly taken out the wrong course book from the library and, because of this, hadn't correctly done the homework that would later be marked by my peers in class. Wait, it gets better – with the results read aloud in front of the entire class, people I'd just met, whom I really wanted to befriend. Embarrassed, yes. Did I return to the class? No!

That's the lizard brain right there. In fact, my college experience was incredible and, without a doubt, some of the best years of my life to date. The freedom, my surge in self-esteem, the fashion experimenting, the fashion disasters, the girlfriends I still hang out with and love to this day. All in all, so much positivity to share with you.

Yet, for some reason, I'm recalling that one gut-wrenchingly embarrassing experience. I can still feel the blood rushing to my cheeks as it became clear the answers being shouted out did not match anything I'd written down. The penny dropped with an almighty thud, and I felt sick as a pig.

I can still picture exactly where I was in the room. With psychology not taught in high school, the classes were always oversubscribed, and the room was full. I think we all wanted to feel like grown-ups and had watched way too many American teen shows and wanted to emulate this sophisticated lifestyle and brag to our families that we were taking Psychology 101. I was perched at the end of the table with the classroom door behind me (a quick exit at least as the feeling of wanting the ground to swallow me up deepened). My eyes bounced from one student to another, and my heartbeat pounded faster and faster, as though I were watching a car crash in slow motion but had absolutely zero control of what was to come. Slowly my gaze edged its way closer to the person who had my homework in their hand, all eyes on me as my 'nul points!' was announced. Fuuuuuckkk!

I didn't get it. My big sister, Stephanie, had flourished when she took the class years before and was always bragging about her success and love of the subject. Yet here I was, making a pig's ear of it on the first bloody day. Tears rushed to my eyes as the whole class looked at me with a mixture of disbelief at my idiotic result, woven in with a look of pity. All I could wish for in that moment was for someone else to have somehow made the same mistake.

My point is, I bet if you take a second right now and think of a moment in your life that has stuck with you, it will most likely be a bad experience as opposed to one of your achievements. Wouldn't it be great if, instead, we saw every life moment the same, even the bad ones, irrespective of how much they hurt or caused pain? If we could look back in a way that allowed us to grow and learn to be at peace?

Retelling this story made my stomach do somer-saults, but it also made me giggle. Why? Because that

Samantha was a complete worry-wart who spent a lot of time with her head up other people's arses, grappling for their approval. She was a sweet, caring and pure soul, but she didn't believe in herself. She was unaware she was incredible, an inspiration, hard-working and a darn successful boss bitch in the making. And also that studying psychology was perhaps her sister's journey, not hers.

That moment had to happen because, although bloody humiliating, it pushed me to pluck up the courage to say that, at that moment in my life, psychology wasn't right for me. It pushed me to take sociology, a subject I wanted to take and one that would play a huge role in shaping who I am today. I was setting boundaries instead of suffering in silence. I had a different path to take. My path. It also proved useful years later when I became a teacher. I was clear I would never use this style of teaching, one that puts individuals on the spot in front of their peers. About that, I was adamant.

We need to embrace who we are and drown out the noise from others. What we should be doing, if we are true to ourselves and really want to 'live our best life', is to stop blaming our circumstance for our behaviour, attitude or situation. It's easy to think others view us as 'abnormal' or wrong and to internalise that feeling. When that happens, we become the labels they ascribe to us. It happens in families all the time. He's the shy one, or she's the gregarious one. When this happens, we often find ourselves moulding into the label. I'm not saying it's easy to move away from these labels but once we strive to redefine who we are and start to be proud of ourselves, we can build on that feeling. It's rather like exercise. The more we do it the easier it becomes.

It isn't as easy as one, two, three – and I'm certainly not perfect in any way, shape or form. Nor am I striving for perfection, which is such an abstract and relative term. For me, being the person I am, I strive to feel proud, happy and content in my own skin. I am also someone who thinks less about what others think of me while doing things that give me joy. I'm trying to live my best life and, by golly gosh, I actually think I'm on the path to achieving this.

I laughed out loud when I was asked to write a book on my life. Me, sharing with others how to be a functioning adult? I laughed not because I was being modest or necessarily doubted my capabilities. It just made me giggle because most days I feel like I'm 14, drowning in the responsibilities of adulthood and making really daft mistakes. I mean, I still forget to look right and left when I cross the road in my electric wheelchair and the other day I threw my knickers in the bin instead of the washing machine. I also still sleep every night with a stuffed rabbit named Bunny, who is dishevelled, has one eye and is gender neutral. Once a chocolate-coloured stuffed toy with white tufts of hair and a fluffy white tail, Bunny is now almost completely bald. Bunny no longer resembles a rabbit, but rather a misshapen poo that frankly stinks of my sweaty armpit and dribble because, oh yes, at the age of 36 I seem to have started to dribble in my sleep.

But Bunny, like any comforter, was my dearest and, dare I say, still is my most prized possession. If I position a floppy ear under my nose and inhale, a wave of calm washes over me. While we are in confessional mode, bear in mind that this is the same rabbit I used to masturbate with from a young age. From that role, I retired the poor sod once the first eye fell off. It no longer seemed fair.

So, as you can probably guess by now, I am by no means an expert in life lessons or a qualified life coach. This book is not a blueprint on living your best life. I feel blessed you are taking your time to hear my story and, who knows, maybe it will resonate and make you feel inspired in some way. At the least I hope you get a laugh out of my numerous mishaps and at the very best I hope you can take away some of the life tools I've been using along the way. So where better to start than when things go hideously wrong?

3

What to Do When Things Go Tits Up

'Life is tough my darling, but so are you.'

Stephanie Bennett-Henry

One would have thought that by now I would be used to expecting the unexpected, you know, life's little curveballs. I mean, you don't break over 200 bones and not learn to be on your guard. The truth, however, is that I don't wake up each morning, glance at my wheelchair and think, 'Well, today's maybe the day I break another bone, so batten down the hatches, we're in for a rough ride.' Gosh, if I had that mindset, I'd buy a jumbo-sized roll of bubble wrap on Amazon and go to town.

On a subconscious level, I'm always on high alert, like a mother sitting bolt upright when she hears her baby stir in the night. I have what could be described as an internal safeguarding radar, constantly assessing risks in my environment. I'm pretty sure everyone with osteogenesis imperfecta comes with one at birth. I'd like to think that it's positioned right between the sternum, where our wishbone lies. The wishbone is the universal symbol for those who have brittle bones condition because the hope is that one day the only bones to be broken would be those at Christmas when you're making a wish on the turkey.

The only time I ever think about breaking a bone is when I am being idle-minded, thinking about something really unimportant, and reach out, for example, to grab a cup of tea, not noticing that I am teetering on the edge of my wheelchair, moments away from crashing to the floor. Then, my body jolts, tingles and I feel a wave of nausea, my heart in my ears and my cheeks flaming. 'Bloody hell, Sam,' I'll scold myself, 'that was close, you idiot,' before resuming what I'd been doing as though I hadn't just been moments away from a trip to A&E or worse.

You see, the quirkiness of the condition means it's so darn unpredictable. Bone fractures are sporadic and, in many ways, have no pattern or logic. I've been thrown from my wheelchair onto the pavement without even a grazed knee while, on the other hand, I've sneezed and cracked a rib. One New Year's Day I forgot to turn off my morning alarm and at 7am sharp heard the demanding jingle. I immediately turned over in bed, desperate to silence the bastard thing, and, in my haste, snapped my collarbone in two, waking the whole house with my screams. Oh, the irony.

Apart from moments like these I feel pretty invincible. Good job, too, or I'd never leave the house. Sometimes when I talk about my condition or the pain I go through it feels as if I'm talking about someone else. 'Gosh, you must be so brave! That must be so painful,' people might say. Normally, I respond with a coy smile because their comments are often littered with patronising, ableist undertones, or I simply say, 'Yeah, I suppose.' But I'm detached from the words that come out of my mouth, detached from the trauma, and I certainly don't dwell on the prospect of future pain and distress. It's like I'm talking not about me, but about a character in a movie. Maybe there's an element of denial, but I think it's more of a coping mechanism, just like when women give birth they're supposed to forget all the pain of childbirth otherwise they wouldn't pop another one out and that would be the end of the human race.

So, sometimes, when the unexpected occurs and the reality of my condition makes its presence felt, the fragility of life comes crashing towards me like a wrecking ball and I'm thrown totally off balance. In those moments, I feel so vulnerable and terrified. The precariousness of my situation feels so close to home, and I'm left with the reality that life is fleeting. Every dice with death – or at least a long stint in a plaster cast – puts my plans temporarily on hold and acts as a reset button on my life. At these times, I sit and ask myself: am I truly making the most of it?

I guess we are all faced with these toothache moments. We swear we will become a better person – or at least floss daily – and pray to any god who'll listen.

We promise to do more volunteer work or never take our partner for granted. Anything to get rid of the agonising pain. Then a few days pass, the pain subsides, and we go back on our merry way, forsaking all the life changes we'd vowed to adhere to.

But what if you stood by your word? What if you saw through all your promises? What would your life look like and would you, in fact, be living your best life? The über-goal would to be live true to yourself 365 days a year, not waiting for pain or heartache to reset your life morals and values. Practising mindfulness and living in the moment is, however, fucking difficult. I mean, I adore Eckhart Tolle (for one he is a fellow German and, two, I love anyone who laughs at their own jokes) but, come on, we aren't all enlightened geniuses.

Tolle's first book, *The Power of Now*, is a great start for anyone who wants to reprioritise their life. His teachings are great for bringing stillness into the hectic world in which we're all forced to live. When some hear the word 'mindfulness' it is Eckhart Tolle's name that springs to mind. For others it just makes them think it's a load of woke, pretentious nonsense. Perhaps, like me, you might sit comfortably between the two viewpoints.

My 'mindfulness' journey is still in its infancy and I'm by no means an expert on it but, hand on heart, I'm already reaping the benefits of this practice. Many spiritual scholars say that happiness and a fulfilled life lie in not dwelling on the past or worrying about the future, rather understanding that the only thing we truly have is the present. The moment just now. Therefore, we should try to take time to stop and be in that moment. Take in all the emotions we feel right now and be grateful for what we have in the present.

Anyone who has experienced therapy for anxiety such as cognitive behavioural therapy (CBT) will already be familiar with the concept of mindfulness and learning to become in tune with your present state.

When mindfulness was raised during my own CBT, I became almost angry that the therapist would 'prescribe' mindfulness as a fix for my anxiety. My worries are not irrational or hypothetical, rather they are based in my lived experience. My anxiety flares up from external factors outside of my control. I don't wake up each morning thinking 'today is the day I'm going to break a bone', but I do think and plan my life to avoid unnecessary 'risks' – such as how can I navigate an incompetent taxi driver who is helping me into a vehicle or get past roadworks blocking dropped kerbs? I can't not think about the future.

How, then, can *I* practise mindfulness? I always have to be one step ahead. Finding ways to safeguard myself from future barriers, growing old, managing loss of function, battling benefit changes. Initially I saw mindfulness as a rather privileged and ableist approach.

The pandemic has meant that I have spent the past two years, like many of us, in relative isolation. I've taken this time to get to know me and what I want in life. What makes me happy. Part of this has been revisiting the idea of mindfulness. Starting with downloading the *Calm* meditation app (other apps are available) and listening to a guided meditation each night. It soon became clear that how I viewed mindfulness was all wrong.

The practice is not asking you to live in a blissfully ignorant state in which you cannot think about the past or future at all. In fact, mindfulness encourages an openness about discussion of death, as it is often seen as the best way to awaken us to the preciousness of life.

Mindfulness is the practice of simply slowing down, looking around and embracing what we have right now. Letting go of past traumas or future fears even if just for a few minutes. To give our body and mind a moment of peace. To take a deep breath and to smile. Oprah Winfrey said, 'Every day brings a chance for you to draw your breath, kick off your shoes and dance. So let this be that gentle, loving reminder to seize the moment right in front of you. Savour it, pour every ounce of yourself into it, devote everything you have to it as it's the only one you ever truly have.'

Now whenever I'm feeling overwhelmed or unworthy, I stop. I breathe. I take in what's happening in that moment and I take note of my emotions. I ask myself whether I'm overwhelmed because of what's happening to me in that second or whether it's a result of something that hasn't yet occurred? Or am I replaying a conversation from weeks ago? Often when I have my mindful moment, I identify that in the present I am safe, loved and grateful. Most of the time I also have a Sphynx cat on my lap or head purring loudly and of course that always helps.

I'm not trying to convert or convince anyone to start to practise mindfulness because I had to come to the conclusion on my own terms, in my own time. I would say that taking these baby steps has already improved my anxiety – not fixed or eradicated it, but simply allowed me to regain control and be pragmatic. The journey of consciousness is different for everyone, but I hope that by sharing my own experience it may inspire you.

For now, though, let's work with what we have and turn cluster-fuck moments into life-changing, life-affirming lessons.

As far back as I can remember I've attended a children's hospital that specialises in treating patients with osteogenesis imperfecta. All my major operations have taken place there, including having telescopic rods inserted into my legs when I was two and then again when I was four (a technique once called 'kebabbing' because the surgeons would remove the femur and tibia bones, chop them into bite-sized pieces and slide them back onto a telescopic rod similar to a car aerial – just like you prepare a chicken skewer to pop on a barbecue). Medical advances have enabled a much less invasive procedure nowadays, but I kind of like 'kebabbing'. It certainly has the shock factor, and it gives you one heck of a party story. Plus, I've got a super-sexy scar to boot.

I'd go as far as to say that the children's hospital is a home from home. I appreciate that sounds rather strange as most people think of hospitals as unpleasant institutions, places to be avoided at all costs. But in many ways, I loved it. What's not to love as a kid, when anything out of the norm could quickly and easily be turned into an adventure. Most of the time I got to skip school, excitedly telling my fellow classmates that I wouldn't be in classes tomorrow because 'I'm going to the hospital'. I liked having an air of mystery around me, and the innocence of young children meant my being different was something to be intrigued by, not something to be feared or rejected. I see this now even as an adult, as it's often the case that young children approach me in the supermarket.

'How old are you?' they might ask.

'I'm 36.'

'But you are so tiny! Why do you look funny?'

At this point their little faces contort as they try to unpick what they see before them.

'I've got poorly bones,' I'll reply, 'so I don't grow like you. That's why I use a wheelchair. Pretty cool, hey?'

They often smile and simply accept what they have been told; no judgement, no bias. They see me for who

I am. Often, however, as they turn on their heel to head back to where they came from, a parent or guardian will approach out of nowhere, all in a frenzy, to apologise, dragging the child off and scolding them as they go, as though their curiosity had caused offence. No one is born with hate or bias. We are moulded over time.

Often, trips to hospital turned into a family day out. The whole family would wake up early, then take the treacherous, snaking paths winding in and out of the heather moors, sometimes pulling up to eat the peanut butter sandwiches Mum had prepared the night before. The roads were more terrifying than the prospect of surgery as I always felt as if the car would fall off the edge. As I was so small, I never really got out of a booster seat. Because my hips are bowed I can't sit with my legs together and I remember the sides of the child seat rubbing. It was so uncomfortable. My dad would chain smoke so kept the sunroof open and his very blond, naturally spiky hair would fly out of the top. I'd have Bunny with me and one of his ears would be jammed under my nose. I loved it when Dad had a cigarette as the smoke filtered through Bunny's ear and I adored the smell.

Even when I had operations, I still enjoyed the whole experience. I felt special and I got to chat with other kids my age. I chose which meals I wanted each day from the cafeteria menu, which always included jelly and ice cream, a luxury I certainly did not have back home every dinnertime. I relished the attention and having a fuss made of me. I received so many gifts from family and friends, which would really irritate my sister, Stephanie, much to my delight. There was never a dull moment.

I remember one time when my sister swung back on her chair and accidentally hit the alarm. A loud siren quickly followed, then the commotion of the crash team rushing into my room. Safe to say my sister got a good bollocking from my father, all adding to the fun experience for me, of course!

As I grew older, the hospital became a place for me to show off my charm and charisma, along with a hint of teenage arrogance. 'Thanks, but I know how to get to the X-ray room.' 'Oh, I come here all the time.' 'Yes, that's my file just behind you – the really thick one.' I always felt so grown up. This was my turf and I loved to show everyone how confident and articulate I was, something that wasn't always appreciated back at school because being different and confident with it was a sure way to get bullied.

The kids at my primary school were lovely. They were intrigued by me. We were friends. I was one of them. But I went to high school with a whole different bunch of friends who saw me as an outsider, a weirdo, a loser, someone not to be entertained. I often felt stunted in the real world, undervalued and misunderstood. I had such a loud voice, so when people tried to intimidate me, I would give it right back to them. It didn't always work in my favour, though. I didn't ever feel like a victim as I would always speak up, but some of the kids would kick the back of my wheelchair in class or one girl would call me Mini-Me, which I think was a reference to the Austin Powers film that had just come out. I would feel sick going into class with any girl who might antagonise me.

In hospital they got me, at least on a medical level. The doctors would include me in conversations and not dumb down their jargon. I was the centre of attention and that suited me just fine. Regular hospital visits were part and parcel of my life, so I didn't think twice when I received my annual check-up letter. I knew the score: take the long trip, sit around for a few hours, have a chat with my specialist, talk through any aches and pains, and Bob's your uncle and Fanny's your aunt, we'd be back home again by teatime. This, however, wasn't always how it played out.

It is 2005 and I am studying at Lancaster University, doing German, French, Sociology and European Studies. I know, right? Quite the academic. A family friend, Nadia, is studying languages at a university close to the hospital so we had planned to meet after my appointment.

'It won't take long,' I tell her, 'so if you want to wait with us that would be fine, instead of hanging around outside.'

It always rains on our hospital trips and I can't have her standing in the cold, but in all honesty the prospect of Nadia getting caught in the bad weather isn't my main concern. Rather, I see an opportunity to show her a glimpse of my world and maybe a chance to show off just a tad.

We are bundled into a packed waiting room, where a large whiteboard states which doctors are running behind, something that always annoys me because when *you* are five minutes late, they kick up a fuss.

The board is a clear marker that this is indeed a hospital but looking around it resembles more of a kindergarten: there are toys scattered about, miniature chairs everywhere and a games console bolted to the wall, all in an attempt to mask the fact that this is a place where sick children come. Scanning the room, I am by far the oldest one here. Anyone who has regular medical treatments will testify that children's services are far superior to the adult ones. Kids get funding for wheelchairs, equipment or physiotherapy at the drop of a hat, but somehow as soon as you hit 18 it is as though a miracle has occurred and you no longer need the assistance or medical attention you did just 12 months ago. The danger is that once you transition from childcare to adult services you can almost fall through the net. I knew that all too well so there was no way I was leaving without a fight.

'Samantha Renkeeeeeeee . . .' Bloody hell, no one pronounces my name right. 'It's a silent "e",' I mutter under my breath. With an overly cheerful smile, the nurse points in the direction I should be heading in. With Mum and Nadia in tow, I enter the small consultancy room, greeted by a familiar face – my doctor, Professor Bishop. Again, I scan the room briefly. There are normally a few more bodies: student doctors or a nurse. Then my eyes lock on a face I am not familiar with; his blank expression does not fill me with ease.

'Hello, Samantha, this is the surgeon who is here to talk about your spine.'

The hairs on the back of my neck prick up. If there is one thing I hate, it is talking about my back. I hate it with a passion, with every ounce of my being. If I could have shoved my fingers in my ears and shouted 'LA-LA-LA, I can't hear you!' like infants do when they refuse to listen to their parents, I would have. It is the one thing that triggers feelings of insecurity and makes me feel ugly, undesirable. A reminder that I am 'disabled', which at the time was still very much a dirty word.

On the outside I appeared to be a very self-assured, confident young woman. But scratch my surface slightly and you'll see a broken and hurt individual holding on to feelings of internalised ableism. Years of people telling me I can't, I won't, I shouldn't. Rejection from my peers and boys, all saying that my life, my body isn't normal. I am incapable, unnatural or something almost grotesque.

Nothing bothers me as much as my spine. I've always used a wheelchair and I've always had scars on my body from operations as an infant and I've never much grown past the size of an average four-year-old, but my back, my curve, was new and in my mind it made me stand out more. The thought of someone noticing my curved spine and calling me hunchback or Quasimodo was too much for me to bear.

Up until the age of ten, my spine had been perfectly straight and solid but then it seemed, almost overnight, to bend, twist and curve. It's not uncommon for people who have osteogenesis imperfecta to develop curvature of the spine as well. Scoliosis is when there is an 's'-shape curve; kyphosis is the more common 'c' shape. I had scoliosis but, although it had been on everyone's radar for the past few years, there never seemed to be any urgency to do anything about it. I, on the other hand, was mortified and my urgency was for it to piss off and disappear.

I would do my best to pretend it wasn't there, only to be reminded of it by my mum and my sister telling me to 'sit up straight'. I'd keep my hair long and always ask my mum, 'Does my back look bad in this top?' I'd often avoid looking at myself side-on in the mirror because the protrusion of my back and rib cage was very apparent. I resented it too because I was such a fashionista and the curve in my spine meant that clothes just didn't sit properly. It's a shame I can't go back in time and tell my younger self that it wasn't my body that was wrong, it's the designers who don't embrace diversity.

Back in the consultancy room, I feel sick with embarrassment. I don't want to talk about my back, never mind in front of a friend. Hats off to anyone who's a doctor or surgeon – you have my utmost respect and rightly so – but many could use a lesson in tact, in my view. Without hesitation, the surgeon whips out a bundle of X-rays of my spine, pinning them to a wall-mounted lightbox for all to see.

'So, as you can see,' he says, 'your scoliosis is rather advanced. What I'm proposing is that we operate to straighten you out a little.'

Just like that. One would have thought he was talking about something mundane, like what he bought from Tesco's the night before, not the fact that my spine was completely fucked, and my vertebra were twisted round like a snake coiled around its prey.

All the cockiness and bravado I had displayed just moments ago in the waiting area, my blasé attitude, vanishes in a moment. All I can hear is my heart pounding. *My God, poor Nadia wasn't expecting this*, is my first thought. I can see her from the corner of my eye. At the best of times, she is quiet, softly spoken and demure. Now she seems almost paralysed and as red as beetroot. My mother is out of my eyeline, luckily for me, as I try desperately to hold back the tears. I know if I even glance at her, I won't be able to contain myself.

Then comes the anger. 'Why now?' I ask curtly. Stubborn Samantha, who has served me well in the past, creeps in. 'I'll stop you there,' I say. 'I'm at university and can't just up and leave for an operation.'

Can't they see how much of an inconvenience this all is? Nope, I'm not doing it – end of conversation. I sure as heck am not about to let the dark cloud that has plagued me for years put a halt to my life. Continuing to pretend it isn't there is working just fine for me. Why do they have to go and ruin it?

'Of course, it's your decision, Samantha,' the surgeon says. 'We can hold off until after your studies, but normally we are hesitant to operate on curves of this severity. The longer we leave it, the more we run the risk of not being able to operate at all. It's important to know that these curves will diminish your life expectancy.'

Sorry? What? How long are we talking? Wow, what a shitstorm of a day this is turning into!

No one had ever said that brittle bones came with a sell-by date. I don't want to die. I am meant for great things. I just need time.

'If the curve continues at this trajectory, you will see a drastic reduction in lung capacity, meaning life expectancy could be as soon as your early forties.'

I have a buzzing in my head and feel as if I'm in a film. It is a bit like the start of *Casualty* when it's all a bit blurry. My ears are ringing and I'm feeling really flushed. The surgeon is very calm and he strikes me as a little arrogant. He is very matter-of-fact.

Forties, I think. Isn't that when life starts to get exciting?

'Well, bloody hell, I guess that's that then,' I tell him. 'When do we operate?'

T'was the night before Christmas (nope, hang on, that's a different story) but it is the night before my hospital admission, 48 hours before my life will change irreversibly and I'll undergo a spinal fusion to correct my severe scoliosis and, yay, prolong my life expectancy.

Operations like these are scheduled months in advance so the build-up for me is reasonably manageable as I go about my busy daily life. Uni is all-consuming and – as a prolific worrier – the stress of coursework and exams are a welcome distraction from the looming operation.

Yet, as I lie in my bed, after months of putting thoughts of the operation to the deepest back of my mind, they resurface, whooshing down like a swarm of wasps attacking every inch of my body all at once. *Shit, I suppose this is happening then?*

I am living with my mother at my stepfather's home. He and my mother got together a few years after my dad died.

His house is a beautiful, converted cowshed, now a luxurious home, with high ceilings with beams and skylights in each room. One is positioned directly above my bed. Under normal circumstances, I loathed it waking me up prematurely, the light so intense in the mornings I am forced to wear an eye mask. But tonight is different. I appreciate being able to lie back and gaze at the moon and the stars, January winds pushing the clouds across the sky.

I wonder if it's too late to change my mind. *Do you think the doctors will be pissed off with me? Maybe they got it wrong? Maybe I'll outlive their expectations? No, don't be daft, Sam, you've got this. It's too late now to back out now.* So many things have been put into place. Plus, I can't deny that the pain in my back has worsened, the curve tilting my body to the right. I am like a blonde Leaning Tower of Pisa, my ribcage pushed so far out that my skin isn't enough to cushion the bone any more. Sleeping on my right side is unbearable. My spine is so compressed that I don't even have a neck, something I feel so self-conscious about.

That night I pray. I pray a lot. I don't do it often. I was brought up Catholic, the German side of my family all practising Catholics. Every time we visited my Oma, I'd have to play along and convince her that we were equally as devout in the UK. It's not that I didn't believe in a god, more that I just didn't know if I believed in *that* God. Nevertheless, I think to myself, there is no harm in reaching out to whoever may be listening.

This is my prayer. 'Dear God, please keep me safe when I go into hospital. I really don't want to die. I actually really love my life and I want to see what happens next. Also, Mum has already lost her husband and I don't think she will survive if I pop my clogs too. I know I've just asked you to keep me alive, but can I be cheeky and also ask for me not to become paralysed too, a high probability with such an extensive operation? I mean, I know I'm already in a wheelchair and I know I'd cope, but honestly, I think I'm already jumping through enough hoops, don't you?'

My mind starts to wander as it often does. It is why I'm so rubbish at meditation. Shit, if I do lose sensation from nerve damage, I may also not be able to feel my bean any more either. I'd best have a final wank – the wank of all wanks – to go out with a bang, so to speak. I won't be able to do it in hospital because Mum will be on the pull-out mattress next to me and that's all kinds of weird!

I lie in bed toying with the idea but my superstitious mind is working overtime, convincing me that my actions will have consequences and will directly impact the outcome of my operation. Internalised Catholic guilt. Nope, can't do it. I mean I've just been talking to God. I can't now just drop my knickers and go to town! But if I don't do it and something does go wrong, I may never get the chance again. The stakes are too high either way. But ultimately I need any divine intervention I can lay my hands on.

I add to my prayer. 'Okay, God, so here's the deal. If I promise not to masturbate tonight, do you promise to keep me safe in the operation?'

I suddenly feel really old at the children's hospital. I am 19 and my 20th birthday is just days after my operation. The halls are covered with brightly coloured murals of clowns and underwater fish scenes, all of which just seem so juvenile now. In a place that once comforted me and now terrified me, getting a teddy bear from the tuck shop isn't going to cut it any more and jelly and ice cream have lost their appeal.

The night before I had stayed up late. I have never been a night owl and normally I'd be in bed by 10pm sharp, but this night it was closer to midnight. I rolled up and down the ward. I'd been given my own private side room, and I knew I'd be stuck in there for the weeks ahead. I wanted to chat with the nurses, anything to keep my mind off what tomorrow would bring. The chit chat with my mum had fizzled out hours ago and, in any case, I didn't want to worry her with my own fears. She had the agonising wait while I was sedated to look forward to, something I would not wish on any parent. Also, I'm not the best company when stressed: I'm snappy, agitated and a bloody grump. They say you are horrible to the people the closest to you; well, my poor mother got the brunt of my frustrations, so for both our sakes it was best we were apart.

'The anaesthesiologist would like to have a chat with you about tomorrow,' said one of the nurses with a cheerful smile, the one thing I still appreciated about being in a kids' hospital. Everyone seemed much more upbeat and optimistic. It was contagious. It dawned on me that this had never happened before, not that I could remember anyway, and this operation was the ninth or tenth surgery I'd undergone. Why would she want to talk to me? Should I be worried? Then I realised this time it was different. I was an adult and I had to make all the decisions, including signing the consent form, acknowledging the risks and complications that may arise during and after surgery.

It was no longer the responsibility of my parents, who, up until now, had to make these decisions for me and shoulder the pressure and emotional burden. Under normal circumstances I'd relish any opportunity to be more adult, to be given independence and responsibility, but this was a whole different kettle of fish. I did not want to be the one in charge.

Given that my spine was already crushing my internal organs, squashing my heart into my ribcage, tilting my body, and leaving me with a mere 50 per cent lung capacity, the anaesthesiologist's job became ten times more difficult. She towered over me. She sported a blonde bob, something I too could acquire after my back was straightened, I thought, as I'd finally have a neck and less of a curve.

I felt comfort in the fact that a woman would be by my side during the operation. I was always under the impression that the male surgeons would just see me as a slab of meat, an intricate piece of machinery that was broken and which they would try to fix with their tools, just like your granddad tinkering around in the shed with that broken vacuum cleaner that should have been thrown out but you let him get on with it because it gets him out of the way. As the anaesthesiologist spoke calmly, softly, not in any way patronising but rather with sympathy and respect, I thought to myself, *Everything will be okay tomorrow*. And with that I was able to get a few hours' sleep.

My eyes are cloudy, and my body is limp, but the beeping of the machine next to me lets me know that I am post-op in intensive care.

'Thank fuck!'

My eyes close again and I heave a deep sigh of relief, knowing that I have come through to the other side. Still highly medicated, I sleep peacefully for the next few hours until I am rudely awakened by a nurse feeding me morphine intravenously. I feel like my arm is being set alight. Then my breathing tubes are removed, one of the most unpleasant experiences – like having a hosepipe yanked out of your body. God, I am thirsty.

I doze in and out of consciousness and wake to find my mum to the left of me and Stephanie to the right.

She shoves a tiny mouse soft toy in my face with Sam written on its little jumper.

'Look what I got for you,' Stephanie cries. 'It says Sam!' Thankfully, I am heavily sedated because I really could have punched her. With a morphine drip in my hand, feeling utterly groggy, the last thing I wanted was a squishy mouse stuffed in my face.

'I'm hungry,' I mutter, my voice still hoarse from the breathing tubes. It's the darndest thing, but I am always ravenous after every operation even though I know my body, still pumped with chemicals, won't tolerate anything solid. Yet, having been nil by mouth for more than 24 hours, I crave anything.

'What shall we get you to eat?' Stephanie says.

'McDonald's,' I reply (at least we now know I'm a cheap date).

I'm not sure if it is Mum or Steph who broke the news, but I do know it was probably one of the hardest things they've ever had to do.

'Sam,' I hear a voice say, 'during the operation there was suspected spinal cord damage. They're going to keep you sedated until they know how serious it is.'

I'm sedated, my mind isn't working properly, but a voice in my head is saying, *No, I'm not going to let this happen to me.*

My spinal fusion had lasted exactly 12 hours and, by and large, was a success. My spine was untwisted, my curves made slightly less curvy. I had even grown a few inches and, by gosh, I now had a teeny tiny neck (I still didn't have the heart to cut my hair off into a bob, mind you!). I had, however, lost a lot of blood due to my weak and temperamental arteries. I had to have around seven blood transfusions. It wasn't until I'd been sewn back up and was brought back to consciousness that it had become apparent that all was not good in the hood.

Days later I was handed a piece of paper by my sister. Most of the content was illegible scribble, but in the corner I could just about make out the words: 'Can't move legs'. My heart broke for that Samantha, the one who must have been so confused, scared and alone. The drugs ensured I have no memory of that time, but I do know that I'm a fighter and, when sedated, will often try to pull out my breathing tubes. This time all I did apparently was ask for a pen and paper and hoped for someone to tell me it was all okay.

After any spinal operation, response tests need to be done to check for any neurological damage.

'Can you move your hands, Samantha? Can you squeeze my fingers?'

My upper body responded as it should, but my lower limbs were non-responsive. My observations had been closely monitored throughout and nothing had sparked alarm bells, so all this came as a shock to everyone involved, none more so than the surgeon himself. Still to this day, we joke about how I singlehandedly gave him grey hairs.

I was put back under sedation to prevent any more damage being done until the team could get to the bottom of why I couldn't move my legs. By this time, it was midnight. My family had been informed and the surgeon had been on the phone, waking up all the top spinal surgeons he could think of across the country to ask for advice on how to proceed.

There's always a slim chance of something like this happening when you sign up for anything to do with your spine, but the likelihood of what happened to me was so small it had flummoxed everybody. We were left with two options: remove all the metalwork in the hope of relieving any pressure that it might be causing on my spine, but in doing so sacrificing any possibility of putting the metal frame back in and dashing my hopes of one day getting a birthday card from a royal. The other option was to keep the metalwork in and hope for the best. Perhaps over time, once the swelling began to subside and I began to heal, I would regain movement in my lower body.

I cannot begin to describe how grateful I am still to this day that my family made the decision to keep the metalwork in. My sister, as cool as a cucumber (as she so often is – she's one of those annoying people who can walk into an exam and not even bat an eyelid), told everyone repeatedly that I was going to be fine and there was no need to be worried. The strength of her positivity would rub off on me in the days to come.

Then, less than 48 hours after my operation, we had a glimmer of hope. My big toe started to move. In my mind, this minuscule amount of movement was all I needed to reassure myself of who I was. I'm bloody Samantha Renke, a fighter! For me, it wasn't *if* I'd get better, it was just a matter of *when*.

Now I am back on the ward, back in my room. The lights are not as harsh and it is not as eerily quiet as in intensive care, where the only sound is the beeping from the machines monitoring heartbeats. It is all hustle and bustle on the ward, nurses rushing around, bedpans being brought in and out of rooms, and an elderly lady pushing the tuck-shop trolley. It is a welcome change of scenery and a reminder that life goes on.

Outside, the sky is gloomy, rain dancing on the window. As a winter baby, I've always felt a warmth and comfort from harsh weather, the feeling of being all cosy and safe curled up indoors. Before my operation I'd dreaded being stuck in my room post-op, but now all I can think is how grateful I am to be back.

Mum and Stephanie haven't slept or eaten since my surgery, while I had been blissfully unconscious, unaware of the drama I had caused. They had been the ones worrying, taking charge, making the decisions.

'Just go for a walk or something, get some fresh air. I will be fine,' I beg them, aware of their gaunt and tired faces.

'Maybe we can go to Lakeside?' Stephanie suggests to my mum. It is a shopping mall just a stone's throw from the hospital.

'But we still haven't spoken to the surgeon,' Mum says, worried. We haven't really had a chance to talk to him since I was moved to the ward and was finally able to wiggle my big toe.

'He could be hours yet. Just go. Honest, I'm okay.'

Knowing that they are finally going to get some food inside of them and see the light of day allows me to drift off into a peaceful snooze until I am woken by the surgeon. He has dark circles under his eyes, mirroring his dark hair. He seems young for a surgeon of his calibre.

'How are you feeling, Samantha?'

I muster up my most cheerful reply. 'I'm okay. Did they tell you about my toe? That's good, right?'

The lack of the enthusiasm I desperately needed to hear fills me with dread. He seems controlled, even deadpan as he examines my chart and asks questions about my progress. Why did I tell my mum and sister to leave? I really don't want to be alone right now.

'I will be able to move my legs again, right?' I ask. In my head I have already heard his response. Yes, of course, Samantha. It's all going to be fine. This is just temporary, nothing to worry about. What he actually says comes, then, as an almighty blow.

'Honestly, Samantha, I can't say for sure.'

It's devastating, and my mind is a whirl as he asks me a few more questions then goes on his way. But after he's gone and I have time to reflect, stubborn Samantha returns – the Samantha that can be a real pain in the bum at times. She doesn't like to be told 'no, you can't, you won't'. Underestimate me and see what happens. This Samantha has seen me through hard times in the past and I am glad in this moment that she is back. No more feeling scared, feeling like a victim or hopeless. I have a fire in my belly and my mind is made up. I am going to be fine.

Alone, I try to digest the information before me. Then a figure appears in the doorway. I sigh. Please, not more doctors.

'I'm back, babe.'

The sight of my mum makes me burst into tears. She rushes to me to cradle my head, fearing the worst.

'What's happened?'

'It's just proper shit, Mum!'

Holding my hand, trying not to knock the cannula in my wrist, she reassures me the best she can.

'We'll get through this.'

As she does, something occurs to me. I reach down, moving my nightgown to the side. Mum whispers into my ear, knowing full well what I am investigating.

'Can you feel your little bean?' she asks. We look at each other in horror, neither of us quite believing she has just said this.

'Yes, yes, I can!'

We both sob and laugh all at once. I take it as a good omen.

The next few days are the worst. Under normal circumstances a patient would be encouraged to get up a few days after their operation. The quicker you start moving, the less muscle you waste and the faster you heal. But with my spinal cord damage, I am on complete bed rest. I must be turned regularly to avoid pressure sores, which is just excruciating. I want to scream, 'wank', 'shit', 'bollocks' with every move but stop myself, remembering I am on a children's ward. Behave yourself, Samantha! I settle for groaning and random other sounds instead.

There is a constant flow of doctors and nurses in and out of my room and, because I am an unusual case – the one that went 'wrong' – I become a subject of gawping by student doctors and the like. I feel like a fish in an aquarium; an experience that is exhausting. I just want to sleep. I am feeling extremely weak, and my body rejects any solid food, even soup. I am not going to be getting that McDonald's anytime soon and, just to add insult to injury, the stress has brought on my period prematurely!

The ironic cherry on top of the cake comes on my birthday, which goes from bad to worse. I turn 20, but it is not the celebration I had had in mind. The only thing that seems to play on television is *Deal or No Deal* and I bloody hate it but can't even move to turn the blasted thing off. My room is littered with cards, an odd mixture of Get Well Soon and Happy Birthday.

I have had no visits from friends at this point. Being in hospital means it isn't a quick, five-minute car drive from my hometown of Leyland and I've learned over the years that people don't do well with pain and suffering. Many would rather just enjoy the happy and bubbly Samantha, not the broken-boned, crying-and-in-agony one. My birthday goes by just as any other day. I am not really in the mood for celebrations. In fact, by this point, I have become increasingly impatient. I start to feel somewhat better within myself and don't understand why they won't just let me sit up, even a few inches.

Sod them, I'm going to do it anyway. With all my might I try to raise myself up in bed but to no avail. It is the strangest sensation. Mentally, I am instructing my body to rise, to go, but it is unresponsive, heavy, weighed down, as though my mind and body are completely separate entities.

I haven't had a proper wash for days and I stink. You know it's bad when you can smell your own putrid BO. To top it all off, my hair is falling out, or seems to be. Mum had put in two French plaits on either side of my head so that my long blonde mane wouldn't get in the way during surgery, but we'd forgotten that my skull would be suspended with wires and bolts. I was face down during surgery with my head over the edge of the operating table, which had to be clear enough to support the respirator, hence the suspension. The holes in my head meant that those areas had to be shaven, as well as the nape of my neck. We are blissfully unaware of this, until my mum decides to freshen the plaits up and unravels them, grabbing clumps of shaven hair as she goes. My hair, however, isn't the high point of my birthday extravaganza.

Anyone who's had an operation is usually fitted with a catheter, meaning one can pee without physically going to the loo. It's usually removed not long after surgery, but mine has been kept in place because of my special circumstances. The catheter goes up the urethra and a small balloon is inflated in the bladder to hold it in place. Wouldn't you know it, my balloon got deflated by accident.

The need to pee isn't a sensation you are supposed to have with a catheter. It is decided the sensation I'm feeling is a positive sign my nerve endings are working down below and the catheter is to be left out to see if I can pee normally.

'Drink plenty of fluids,' the nurse says.

Stephanie picks me up some cranberry juice. 'Here you go, sis. Help to flush you out.' She shoves a plastic cup and straw in my face.

'I haven't got thrush, you plonker!'

The hours go by: more juice, water, but no pee. I feel like I need to go but every time I try . . . nothing. They discuss whether the obstacle is purely psychological, which I find insanely patronising and infuriating. I know something is amiss and it isn't because I have stage fright. The hours continue to tick by, and my bladder grows and grows. I plead for the catheter to be reinserted but it's a procedure normally done under sedation and not one of the nurses on the ward appears to be able or available to perform it. I've experienced pain in my life but I'm telling you that, without a doubt, having a bladder the size of a grapefruit and not being able to go to the bathroom is the most excruciating pain I've experienced. I wouldn't wish it on my worst enemy.

It is now getting close to 11pm and it has been arranged for someone from intensive care to catheterise me again. By this point I am screaming out in agony, not caring how loud I am. The pain is unbearable! My mother, who is a nurse, trained in Germany, demands action. I'll never forget her 'Denglisch' accent. My mum rarely raises her voice, but she is so pissed off and can't bear seeing me writhe in pain.

'This is bloody ridiculous,' she screams. 'Give me a catheter. I'll do it!'

Finally, late into the night, they come to catheterise me once again. The release is immense. Hallelujah! The tension in my room has been insufferable; everyone feeling frustrated, angry and agitated. With my bladder release also comes a sigh of relief from everyone around me.

Keeping a catheter in long term, however, can cause infections so it is suggested we try something else. I meet with a urologist the following night. He tells me he will take me into surgery first thing in the morning and fit me with something called a super pubic catheter. He speaks calmly and with clarity. After all the fuss and agony from the night before, he is a much-needed voice of reassurance.

There are talks that I may not ever be able to go to the bathroom without assistance and that I may have to learn to catheterise myself permanently. But this is something I am not going to give up on and having the urologist believe in me is exactly the support I needed. This catheter will sit externally in the pubic bone area before going through the abdominal wall. A little lever, like one you'd find on a beer keg, will sit just below my tummy. I could try to go to the toilet naturally and, if that doesn't happen, I just open the lever and away I'd go.

I am not too happy about having another procedure, so I opt for it to be undertaken under local anaesthetic instead of another general. With Mum holding one hand and a nurse the other, the urologist inserts a very long needle through my pubic wall. It hurts like a bitch, but I am just relieved that it is one thing I don't have to think about any more. Later that evening I start to get a tingling sensation in my nether region. I have been using the valve to relieve myself, but this time I persist and, yes, we do indeed have lift off! It is as though the floodgates have been opened and for the next hour all I can do is pee. I have gone from not being able to go to not being able to stop.

In all, I spend almost three weeks at the children's hospital. Each day my legs start to move a little more. The first time I sit in my wheelchair I feel as though I have a completely different body. I have the sensation of someone strapping a stiff plank of wood to the back of my neck and my body is getting used to its different shape as the muscles knit back together and my organs shift. The trauma of the operation has been likened to that of a major car crash. It takes the best part of two years for me to feel mentally and physically well again.

It also took over a year for me to retrain my bladder. Every time I got a particular sensation, I knew I had to find a toilet fast. It was honestly agony for me as a young woman getting to grips with mild incontinence. I refrained from going out as often and I worried about body odour.

In the room adjacent to mine in the hospital was a young girl who had been brought in after a car crash that left her paraplegic. I often think about her; who was she and what has she achieved? I hope she has the same fire in her belly to prove everyone wrong that I did.

I went back to see the surgeon for a number of years after my spinal fusion for check-ups and so forth. Your body can be an absolute arse if it chooses and can reject the metalwork even years later, leaving you that last little element of the unexpected, which as you know I'm never prepared for, even if by now I really should be.

I've always been in awe of him. He's seen my insides. I'm never going to see them. I wish we'd recorded the surgery. He always looked a little dishevelled, the dark circles under his eyes still apparent along with the strands of grey hair. I knew he had small children; his kids will grow up being so proud of their father.

The night of my operation he never went home; he probably doesn't go home many nights. What a weirdly beautiful sacrifice to make, putting others' needs above your own. I wonder how he went for a pee during my surgery. Did he use one of those devices people take to concerts that they strap to your leg? So many questions left unanswered. Unlike the one he'd asked me over and over again, as though he didn't like my answer or wasn't convinced by what I had to say.

'Samantha, do you regret having the procedure?'

Without hesitation, looking him dead in the eye without even flinching, each time I'd reply: 'Absolutely not!'

I wondered if what had happened with me niggled at him. Was I the odd apple that had somehow ended up in the basket at the organic shop, the one that slipped through the net? He later told me that I had been used as a case study at medical conferences across the globe – the one that just didn't go to plan and no one really knew why.

I laughed. 'I'd do just about anything to be centre stage!'

I mean, safe to say, the whole ordeal was a gigantic clusterfuck. Of course, I would have wanted the operation to run smoothly without any hiccups, without months and months of agonising pain and rehabilitation and long-lasting neurological damage. But I came away from that operation with the best result – I had stabilised my spine. I was out of pain, I had a neck and, above all, I'd extended my life expectancy.

I was so proud of myself for taking the risk, for going through with the operation in the first place, so proud of the strong young woman I'd become. I was proud of returning to university into a different year group with strangers, while my peers were on their year abroad and smashing it.

For some, my surgery may not have been the success it could have been. For me, it was a moment in my life to reconnect with who I was. So strong, someone who can see the light even in the darkest of hours. Dwelling on what should have been doesn't help anyone. I choose to focus on the positives.

Many of us are guilty of focusing on the negatives or our limitations. We obsess about what we think is wrong with our bodies or what we don't have or can't do in life, instead of appreciating what we have, giving ourselves a pat on the back for what we have accomplished, our achievements and the many amazing attributes we possess. There will always be ups and downs and the unexpected around the corner, but we must not lose sight of the good.

The operation took a lot out of me, mentally and physically. I came away feeling as though I'd been given a new start in life, without reduced life expectancy looming over my head. The trauma reminded me of how bloody fabulous and resilient and strong I am. It almost took away any fear I had for those future curveballs that would inevitably be thrown my way. Most importantly, it sparked something inside of me: the stubborn, or shall I say resilient and determined, Samantha, who didn't take no for an answer. She would be the catalyst that ignited the flame within and gave me the nudge to break free from social constraints and to start living exactly how I wanted to without asking for anyone's approval.

Sometimes, then, we need to be pushed to our limits to remind ourselves how remarkable we truly are.

Every hurdle, every trauma that came with the operation showed me what I'm capable of. It pushed me to believe that I am a fighter, and I could turn tragedy into positivity. I came away with a new respect for my body and mind. If I'd come through all this, then what else could I take on? The operation had reignited the fire in my belly that had been lost. I felt alive and I wanted to keep pushing.

My future now looked too exciting because I knew, whatever came my way, I would smash it.

It's rare for any of us to go through life without being hit by something we didn't see coming. Whether that's illness, loss, a break-up, job loss, quarrels or any other of life's dramas. These trials aren't a reflection on us, they are simply part of life. We can, though, try to reframe our thoughts around these episodes and do our best to use them to recognise our strength and resilience. Then, when the next bad thing happens, we can draw on the fact we coped with the last one.

4

Dare to Dream

'The key to success is to start before you are ready.'

Marie Forleo

A dream is planted in your heart for a reason. It's up to you to see it realised. I'm a firm believer that if something doesn't give you anxiety shits, it's not worth pursuing and, believe me, there's been a lot of that going on in writing this book. Every day we make decisions. Some are tiny, others enormous. What should I wear this morning, poached or scrambled eggs, tea or coffee? Where will I live or what career will I pursue? Shall I watch *Love Island* or spend my time at the gym or, better yet, curl up in bed cocooned in fluffy socks and favourite hoodie and devour a box of Maltesers?

Yet, when we are faced with an important choice, we can often become paralysed by indecision. The anxiety poos in full force. Fearful of making the wrong choice. What if I say yes and it's just not right for me or equally what if I turn an opportunity down and come to regret it later?

The truth of the matter is that decisions are inevitable. Unavoidable. No matter how reluctant we might be, we must make them and then make peace with the outcome. Of course, it's perfectly normal to mull things over. In fact, I'd be concerned if you didn't take time to weigh your options and think about potential outcomes. However, long periods of indecision can leave us stressed and anxious. We've all had sleepless nights, I'm sure, trying to come to a decision. I am the worst, anxiety sweats saturating my bed linen so much I've actually shoved a puppy pee pad under me to absorb the moisture. Sexy, right?

I've learned over the years that it is better to make a choice simply to move forward, even when we're not positive it's the right one. If we aren't moving forward, aren't we simply existing rather than living? So, next time you are faced with a life-changing decision, simply take a deep breath and say, 'I believe in me. I trust me to do what's best.' It is so freeing to follow your instincts and trust your judgement and to simply rest in the relief of having made that decision. Remembering that, even if you end up making the wrong choice, you'll have gained awareness that can guide you in the right direction.

Nothing in life is without value. You know when people say, 'Well, what's the worst that can happen?' The answer is simply that you will never know if you don't at least try. Every choice will bring its pros and cons. The good and the bad. I guess that's why I wanted to write this chapter – I would argue that I am literally living my dream and I want to share with you how I got here. I also want to say that the journey has been no picnic; there was no fairy godmother waving a wand so that everything magically fell into place.

In fact, pursuing my dream has brought me at times to total despair and some of my lowest moments. I have had some of the most exhilarating moments too, from featuring in and co-producing a Boy George music video to appearing in an incredibly famous chocolate commercial and winning the Best Actress award at the Los Angeles diversity film festival for my role in the film *Little Devil*. Despite all that, I have had times of wanting to give up. I've doubted myself. Gas-lit myself. I've felt incredibly isolated.

I went through a period of drinking way more than I should simply because my mind couldn't cope with the pressure I put on myself and the guilt I had for not pushing myself enough. I've also questioned my worth and I still, even now, question whether or not my dream life is all it is cracked up to be. Not to mention spending many months eating three-minute noodles and ready-to-eat couscous because that's literally all I could afford.

Yet here I am writing a book because ten years ago I made a decision. I was strong, I was brave, I stuck to my guns and, ultimately, I changed my life. You see, it's the indecisiveness that can stop us being happy. Living in regret can eat away at us and harm us much more than taking a chance, risking it not going to plan and seeing indeed what's the worst that could happen. Who knows?

That decision you are too scared to make could be a game-changer. There's only one way to find out.

I've never been afraid of my own potential. Ask anyone what I was like as a child and they will, without hesitation, say I was bubbly, confident, cheeky, funny and determined. Yet I was never encouraged to dream big. There I was, a youngster with so much potential and optimism living in a world that couldn't fathom a disabled person succeeding. A world where the adults couldn't see past their own ignorance and narrowmindedness and the negative stereotypes that labelled me a victim. Not a badass individual who could dream as big as she wanted and would succeed at anything she put her mind to.

People say they rarely remember what they dream. I do. I used to have a recurring dream about falling head-first down the stairs of my childhood home, my stomach doing somersaults as I lay sleeping. As someone with brittle bones it didn't end well. I also dreamed I was eaten by a werewolf. I lived on in his stomach, from which I could see out, and I watched on in horror as the beast massacred my entire family and went on a slaughter rampage.

Safe to say, I was an anxious child, a habitual worrier. But not all my dreams ended in misery and bloodshed. Often when I dreamed, I dreamed BIG. I dreamed I was on stage, on television. A pop star, a

Spice Girl. I dreamed I was a teacher. A dancer with a princess dress and tiara, twirling, gliding on the dancefloor. I dreamed of my wedding day, my future children. I travelled the world. I even dreamed that I followed my mum's footsteps and became a nurse. I dreamed I was a witch. Okay, so perhaps watching *The Craft* over and over on a very worn-out VHS had something to do with that one, but my imagination, my aspirations met no bounds.

I had big plans for my future. For me, the world was so full of opportunity and excitement I often wished I would wake up and already be an adult (this time probably because I used to watch the smash hit film *Big*, starring Tom Hanks, on repeat). But most of my early childhood was filled with hope and that made me a rather happy and content child. Until I wasn't. I always knew I was different, but in early childhood I didn't feel it was a bad thing. It was at high school this changed. I only doubted myself when the world made me do it. At high school I felt like an outcast.

But my dreams would always stay with me. In the wonderful haze of my imagination, I am sitting at the back of my school classroom daydreaming, blissfully unaware that the world is going about its business as normal. I can dimly hear the muffled voice of the teacher, the children buzzing around like bees harvesting honey. Crayons and paper in hand, darting across the classroom floor. Some are painting their entire hand in glue so they can peel it off once dried, as a snake might shed its skin. Others are swapping novelty rubbers in the corner under their desks.

I am physically present but mentally I am in my own very beautiful world. I can feel and see everything in the most minute detail, as though watching my dream in high definition. I feel my emotions, as though I am living them there and then. I don't know it at the time, but my visions have started to turn into my own little manifestations. My dreams are not just fantasies. I am creating a reality for myself, visualising my life as I want it to be.

I guess one of the reasons why many of my dreams have come to pass over the years in one way or another is because I didn't create a version of me that was more appealing to others. People are often curious as to how I appear in my dreams. What they really want to know is: have I ever dreamed of walking? In my dreams, am I not in a wheelchair? That's because dreams are supposed to be idealised and liberating, showing the best versions of ourselves.

I think people would like to hear that my dreams freed me from my disability. That I was no longer bound by my wheelchair. Escapism. But the answer is a big fat NO, never. Firstly, I never say I'm bound to my chair. Rather, I use my chair as an extension of me, a tool to liberate me in a disabling world. In all my dreams I've never wavered from who I am. All the success and happiness I conjured up in my mind depicted the funny, confident and outgoing Samantha who happened to be in a wheelchair. Not a cured version with legs as long as a runway; a more palatable version. Just me.

The only difference is that in my dreams I am accepted. I face none of the barriers I face in the real world. I guess my dreams are utopian in the sense that nothing stops me. I never dream of a lift breaking down or someone telling me that no, I can't be a ballerina because I can't walk. Or a doctor, a wife or mother. I just am. No fuss. No restraint. The world is my oyster and I want to devour it with hot sauce.

My innate desire to assert myself as a child allowed me to take a fantasy and visualise myself – my true self – playing the role. I lived my dreams as me. Unapologetic. Unashamed and untarnished by external voices. I wanted everything in my dreams so badly that I willed it so.

All I know is my bloodlust thirst for success and my longing to be the best I could be – not perfect, just my best – meant I did not accept no for an answer. In fact, the word no sparked in me a rage, a passion, a hunger and a desire to prove everyone wrong.

From as far back as I can remember I was so incredibly self-aware. My little body didn't match what was going on inside my heart and mind. I was an old soul. All I can say is that I'm pretty sure this life I'm living right now is not my first rodeo. In fact, a psychic once told me I was a warrior in a past life: a champion, physically incredibly strong. Now, in this life, my physical strength has been taken away because my purpose is to show the world how strong and determined you can be in other ways.

I'm not sure how much of that I believe, but I appreciate its sentiment. In some ways, it is true, because for me, living in a world that doesn't see my potential only turns my determination into strength. It is my unique power.

I cannot begin to put into words how unbelievably frustrating and condescending it is to be seen as one-dimensional. To be seen as a label. To be pigeonholed. Essentially to be stripped of the many layers of my identity and defined by a single one. I have often felt like a cocoon left to wither and fall rather than be nurtured and allowed to blossom, the caterpillar inside emerging into a wonderfully beautiful butterfly, ready to fly off on an adventure.

Even as a youngster I felt like the biggest burden, especially to my family. Burden – a word many disabled people internalise and carry around like a heavy sack of potatoes. We are told that we are a problem. Our condition, our impairment, our chronic illness is a burden on society. As an adult, I've openly been called a drain and a burden, even having a very drunk distant relative insinuate that my own father's death from a brain haemorrhage at the tender age of 38 was largely my fault as he simply couldn't come to terms with having a disabled child; that the stress and guilt caused his demise. Deep down I know this isn't true, but, by gosh, it doesn't mean that I didn't feel like I'd had my heart ripped from my chest at the time. Words like 'burden' repeat on you like acid reflux after a feast.

Growing up with a disability and being around more adults than kids your own age means you grow up super-fast. You also become a master of covert operations. To an untrained eye, I was a cute blonde kid in a wheelchair with oversized multi-coloured glasses from Benetton, playing with a Coca-Cola Kids doll named Carmen, looking like butter wouldn't melt. In reality, I was listening in on the hushed conversations of doctors, physiotherapists, occupational therapists, teachers and teaching assistants, and what I heard often left me feeling confused and sad. The words 'fix', 'overcome', 'challenging', 'different', 'difficult', 'special needs', 'can't' and 'won't' were flung around a lot. I knew being disabled cost lots of money for my parents too – new wheelchairs, equipment and so on – and that my mother gave up her career and home country of Germany to be my full-time caregiver, a move that resulted in a family feud. My Oma did not speak to the family for years because her grandkids had been 'taken away'.

All of this I internalised. It was a lot to shoulder as a youngster. Listen, I don't blame any one of them for seeing me in this way and I don't hold any animosity either. They probably weren't even aware that I was listening.

I was a sneaky little git. I mean, let's face it, we've all 'stumbled' across our parents' dirty magazines or cigarette stash as a child, haven't we? Or, if you had a sister like mine, been shown the Christmas gifts under our parents' bed and told to keep schtum and act surprised on Christmas Day?

The beauty of getting older is that you can begin to empathise with your parents and see them for who they are: people. My parents, who were only in their early twenties at the time I came along, must have been so overwhelmed and under-supported, their only reference for bringing up a disabled child being to follow what society told them. And those, unfortunately for me, were societal values born out of years and years of oppression and marginalisation of the disability community. History shows us that disabled people have always been vilified and victimised. I was simply part of another generation that would shoulder and internalise the harmful stereotypes given by our ancestors. Years of a biased, ableist smog.

If only the people around me could have reached into my soul and realised that I wasn't what they labelled me. I was so much more. I really battled to try to understand why there had to be so much negativity and doubt and, at times, total apathy surrounding my ability to succeed and ultimately live a happy life. Because, in my mind, I had already mapped it out. I just wanted everyone else to be on the same page.

I like to cast my mind back to the little girl who sat cross-legged on the floor each morning, clutching a cup of tea and watching *GMTV*, my morning ritual, with my favourite hosts, Eamonn Holmes and Fiona Phillips. My mum would be brushing my hair and I wouldn't be able to say how much it hurt because I'd feel her wrath. I then fast-forward to the me now living on my own in London, sitting opposite Eamonn Holmes and co-hosting one of his radio shows. The man on my television who I'd watched every day as a child I now call Uncle Eamonn, a pet name I'm pretty sure he's not keen on but is too nice to say otherwise. The man I try to be professional around and act cool with every time we work together, when, in reality, all I want to do is squeeze him tight because he reminds me of that bright-eyed kid who never wavered from believing in herself even when the entire world didn't allow her to dream.

I guess it all comes down to making that decision. The one that skyrocketed me into an upward trajectory, inching me closer and closer to my dream. I'd like to say there was one defining moment in my life that prompted me to take a drastic, life-changing move, but I guess that would be too Disney. The truth is there was a whole host of factors at play. For years, I felt like a jack-in-a-box, suppressed and caged in. Over the years, I slowly wound up and up and, one day, I just sprung out and said to myself, 'Right, things have got to change.' I was that resolute.

My spinal fusion undoubtedly played a huge part; it redefined what living meant. My fragility only drove me to fight harder for life. It had shown me my true inner strength and, in many ways, I felt like I could take on the world. But there was no denying that, although my mind felt so strong, the physical trauma was a lot for this little body of mine and I needed to heal. I had been cut from ear to ear. As I've said before, operations equal trauma.

More than anything else, I needed time. I was learning to regain control over my bladder and to live with the fact that I now had reduced strength in my legs. I had also lost sensation in my feet, my legs, a patch on my right buttock, and the bottom part of my labia. You read that correctly: my labia were numb, one of the effects of spinal cord injury, and there was no guarantee of any of my sensation returning. My neck, although it was now a few centimetres longer, was restricted by the large hook that had been put in place to stabilise the rods. It meant that I now had to sit slightly tilted back so I could lift my neck high enough to see where I was going.

Post-op, my wheelchair no longer felt comfortable either. The extra few inches I'd acquired meant I could barely reach the wheels any more. Then there were the new muscle spasms I was experiencing, another consequence of spinal cord damage. My legs would sometimes involuntarily twitch and move so violently I had to take medication to suppress the jolts so as not to fracture my legs with the force. All of these spasms were accentuated at night, during which I literally looked like I was auditioning for *Riverdance*, my legs flailing about.

Despite all this, I felt as if I had been given a new lease of life. My back pain almost disappeared overnight, and I could now sleep on my right-hand side without my ribs rubbing through my skin. I looked almost unrecognisable; straighter, taller. My clothes fitted me better and my belly piercing was now on a tilt as it had been pierced, pre-op, on a very curved body. My breasts were now much more asymmetric than previously as my straightened body had pushed my chest further out.

So much change, so much healing yet to be done. But I am the first to say that I am the worst for staying still. I craved routine and normality. I returned to university as quickly as I was allowed and had only one thing on my mind – to complete my degree. I was one of only a handful of disabled graduates and I would not let my brittle bones get in the way of my education. I had no desire to become another miserable statistic depicting how disabled people are alienated from higher learning.

The surgery had halted my studies so I returned halfway through an academic year. The friends and peers I'd started my degree with had gone on the mandatory year abroad. As language graduates, this was something everyone was super excited about. It was never an option for me. When I finished college and applied to four universities, I was accepted to them all. When I realised a year abroad was mandatory, I assumed the universities could work around my specific adjustments and I'd make up the credit in another way. Boy, was I wrong. This was the first time in my life I experienced out-and-out ableism. I met with the relevant departments and explained why living abroad for a year with my condition and no support and no accessible housing just couldn't happen. I wasn't being difficult, just honest and pragmatic.

On balance, at that time there almost certainly weren't many people like me applying. The staff probably weren't expecting someone with a severe disability to even apply for a university place, particularly one that included a year abroad. It was an oversight on their part but it was a different time. And yet, even today it's difficult for disabled people to get into university. On an optimistic note, things are gradually getting better, but there are still obstacles for disabled people wanting to access higher education.

Unfortunately, I experienced some rather elitist and pompous attitudes and most of these institutions came back with a verdict of: 'The computer says no!' 'No' isn't in my vocabulary and, although I felt like my world was crumbling, I once again saw this discrimination as a challenge to prove them all wrong.

I gave up on my first-choice university as they wouldn't budge on me not going abroad, and pleaded my case at a number of others. Finally, Lancaster was the only establishment that allowed me to enrol on a language degree without the obligatory submersion year. But it came with a condition. Instead of receiving a German degree I would have to settle for one titled 'Bachelor's Degree in Area Studies German'. What a pile of wank.

I completed my degree with a 2.1 and was one of very few students in my entire year to receive a distinction for German Oral, a skill it was said that can only be acquired by doing the year abroad. Literally drop the mic. Life lesson right there: never back down from what you need. Asking for help or assistance is not a weakness and does not make you any less than anyone else. If other people are too rigid to see the beauty of diversity, then that's their problem, not yours. Keep fighting.

So, there I was, degree in hand but still pretty battered and bruised from the operation and all the complications. Physically and mentally. What now, Samantha? The thought of leaving my education bubble and heading out into the big, bad world was terrifying. I think we all feel a degree of fear when we step into the unknown and leaving the nest can be incredibly traumatic, particularly for someone in my situation. Yes, this strong, badass, young woman was still pretty scared and overwhelmed a lot of the time. I was good at taking one battle at a time, but now I was faced with being a 'proper' adult.

Looking back, I was really not ready to start work or live on my own at the time. I had never even prepared a cup of tea for myself. I guess you're all wondering how that could be possible. You are a graduate, in your twenties and you've never made yourself a cuppa? The truth is, I had a very co-dependent and sometimes rather toxic relationship with Mama Renke. Back then, we were inseparable, two peas in a pod. She even came to uni with me as my support assistant to help me navigate the campus. I wasn't going to be living on campus as I'd never lived on my own and I didn't drive, so having my mum double up as a chauffeur and on-campus assistant just made sense.

Mama Renke, who looks 30 years younger than her actual age, fitted right in. Most of my peers only found out she was my mother in my final year. Still makes me chuckle. Up until this point I had never been challenged to become more independent. It's not like now, with social media, where I can see other amazing disabled people driving or living on their own or on a university campus. Back then, I was very isolated and had no one to inspire me.

One thing I've also become aware of as a disabled person is that information on how you can live like everyone else is kept hush-hush. Car adaptations cost money. Housing is not built with disabled people in mind and costs money to modify. Assistive technology costs money, unless it becomes popular and can be produced for mass consumption. A perfect example is your at-home Alexa, technology that is so perfect for assisted living but which cost the earth until it became popular among able-bodied people. So, for many years, Mama Renke and I remained in the dark about what my life could look like. The alternative would have cost the local authority a lot of money if we'd demanded those gadgets and adaptations. We didn't know that I could become that butterfly, so instead I simply went with the standard narrative I'd been given, which meant that Mama Renke pretty much did everything for me. I felt as though any and all of my life decisions needed to include her. I believed that anything I did would have a huge impact on my mother's life and the responsibility was overwhelming.

It is not uncommon for disabled people to have an incredibly close relationship with their family, specifically their parents or legal guardians. Just to clarify, close doesn't necessarily mean they all get along. The closeness is more of a necessity, a way of surviving. Why? Well, because the support and assistance that should come from the government and local authorities to ensure disabled people have autonomy over their lives is far from perfect – and that's putting it politely. Plus, the lack of funding in the care sector means family members are almost guilted into taking on these roles of

24-hour support networks and caregivers because most parents will do anything for their children. This means the state often takes advantage of them.

These relationships can often become smothering and toxic for everyone involved. That is not to say they aren't filled with love, compassion and goodwill. Mama Renke is undoubtably my BFF. However, my mother was my primary caregiver, who gave up her career, social life, independence and for a time literally lived for me. She became a widow and a mother of two in a foreign country without support, and that weighed heavily on my mind. I felt guilt from both sides – that I had monopolised her life so far and that one day I might leave her. I would often think that if I became independent – if I went off and lived my life – what would this mean for her? What would be her purpose?

The guilt I felt was at times was unbearable and I simply allowed her to do everything for me. It became toxic because I'd even say no to social engagements I'd been invited to because I didn't want to abandon her. The more I put off doing things for myself, the more it scared me to try. I was absolutely playing the role I was given and allowed myself to be infantilised although I was a grown woman.

I did it because I loved her so much. I couldn't leave her. She didn't ask for a child with a disability, and I believed I owed her everything, as fucked up as that now sounds. Back then, I didn't see that my mother owed it to herself to find her own way and build her own life. We leaned on one another in so many ways and, like any co-dependent relationship, it was a vicious circle we simply struggled to get out of.

When I was at university I used my education as a protective shield, one that allowed me to play along with this toxic partnership. I didn't have to concentrate on learning how to cook or how to be more independent, because I was too busy being a student and my studies and my degree came first. It was a good cover, a way to deflect. But now it had come to an end.

Graduation day was looming, and I had no idea what would come next. Then I was presented with a get-out-of-jail-free card. I'm not sure who suggested it, but it was proposed to me that I should continue my studies and get a Postgraduate Certificate in Education (PGCE). With my degree, I could become a modern foreign languages teacher. At the time there was a real shortage for this skill-set, with institutions crying out for language teachers. It meant that not only would I remain in higher learning for another year, but I would also receive a £9,000 bursary. Cha-ching! It was a no brainer. Where do I sign up?

The next year, at Saint Martin's College in Cumbria, is an absolute blur. All I can say is, I take my hat off to anybody who signs up to a PGCE. The course moved fast and it was renowned. We were taught '100 per cent target language' teaching, which basically meant you couldn't use English within your classroom unless you felt a child may be in danger. Then, and only then, could you slip out of your target language and discipline them in English. Excuse my language but, fuck me, it was hard. *You* stand in front of a class of Year Nine kids and not utter a word of English and see how long you have their attention for.

I would wake up each morning around 4 or 5am and prepare my lesson plans, then go to my host school, come home, eat, work on my assignments and sleep. This was my life for a year. The course literally took my spirit and soul. Chewed it for a while, spat it back out and what was left is what I got. A very dishevelled Samantha. Totally not worth £9,000 but it allowed me time to think about my next move. It was the hardest year of my life but, although I wanted to quit more times than I've had hot dinners, the determined little nugget that I am saw it through until the end.

My hard work paid off and, soon after graduation, I landed my first job at a high school. It was, in fact, my second placement and that made the transition so much easier because I'd already been there six months. I stayed at the school for almost three years. For the most part it was a great school, but I was miserable. I had proudly said as a child that I wanted to become a teacher or an actress and this was a part of my dream visualised. Why, then, wasn't I happy? This was supposed to be a vocation, working in an institution I'd remain in for the rest of my working career, but I just didn't feel like I fitted in. I could joke and say I didn't like the kids, but that's not true. I loved how I was a positive role model for them, how I challenged their misconceptions of what disability looks like. I prided myself on being the kind of teacher you'd high-five in the corridor but you'd also know that, in my class, you would be respected and treated as a human, listened to and given room to be yourself.

Clearly, I was projecting all the things I wanted in life within the four walls of my classroom. Nevertheless, I was so unhappy. Was this really it? Was this what my dream really looked like? I yearned for adventure outside the school parameters. I didn't see it back then, but this was simply my first stepping stone towards getting me closer to where I needed to be. Yes, my dream had come to pass but that didn't mean it ended there. I stuck at it for as long as I did because I loved how people saw me when I told them I was a teacher. I stayed in misery because being a teacher meant people treated me the way I'd always wanted to be treated. With respect. It was intoxicating and I didn't want to give up that feeling, even if it meant my mental wellbeing suffered as a result.

When you are disabled, you are constantly bombarded with daily microaggressions, and if you have never experienced one, you may be inclined to believe they don't exist. But, believe me, that's the way they operate: sly and almost unnoticeable unless you are at the receiving end. I remember during one summer holiday break I was clothes shopping when one of the shop assistants engaged in a chat with me. Her whole demeanour and tone of voice was patronising. She was talking to me as if I were a child – physical disabilities are often wrongly associated with impaired intelligence. As the conversation continued, I explained that I was a teacher.

'Primary school?' she enquired.

'No, the stinky, sweaty, hormonal high school ones. I speak several languages too.'

I gloated and boasted because I was using the coping mechanism that I always had – *I'll prove you all wrong*. It worked. Her whole voice and tone changed, her posture straightened and, instead of a crouching over me, she engaged in what I'd call a normal conversation, albeit with her initial shocked expression mixed in with a hint of embarrassment.

As I left the store, I thought, *That'll teach her*. I did that a lot. I conducted my life to prove others wrong, but this attitude was eating away at my own happiness. I became a teacher because I needed to learn what life is like when you live to meet other people's expectations. It was my first step towards understanding where true happiness lies.

It wasn't just my unhappiness at work that led to where I am today. My home life wasn't any easier either. At the time I was living at Mama Renke and her then long-term partner's home. Their own relationship was going through a little rough patch and, for a time, they were 'on a break'. Mama Renke and I moved back into our family home, a bungalow where my sister lived. At first, I loved having Mum all to myself. It had been that way for so long. It felt safe and we knew our roles. But then one day my sister said something to me that hit me so hard.

'If Mum doesn't get back together with her partner, you will never live your life,' she said.

It sounded so cruel and harsh, but she was right. Her words ate at me and made me feel desperate, trapped. The time came to be open with Mama Renke like never before. The conversation was more emotionally charged than I'd have liked. Tears rolled down my face and my voice became raised at times. I remember yelling: 'If we keep going on like this, I will end up resenting you! I need to live my own life and you need to live yours!'

I proposed that she went back to sort things out and I would live with my sister in the bungalow. Relief. I had spoken my truth for once. In that instant, I unburdened myself. After our conversation everything went up and up for me. From that moment on, I remained in the bungalow. My mum patched it up with her partner – to whom she is now happily married – and, would you believe it, I even learned how to make myself a cup of tea.

*

I was now on my way to becoming the queen of independence. Inviting my friends over and cooking for them. Doing my own laundry. Getting in and out of my wheelchair and bum shuffling on the floor into the shower. Taking a taxi each morning to work. I took to my new-found independence like a duck to water. I even applied for a personal assistant who would come and help me with my shopping and basic, day-to-day running of the home so that Mama Renke could be just that: my mum.

With this came a little air of sadness. Why hadn't I done it sooner? The self-flagellation didn't last too long, however, because I was simply having way too much fun. Each day came with a new challenge, but I revelled in them. I no longer feared obstacles. One of the most beautiful skills I have as a disabled woman is seeing the world and all its little challenges and coming up with a solution to master them. Learning to pick things up with my toes, attaching string to doors to pull them to, and hitting light switches way out of my reach with spatulas. I should have been pissed off at how disabling the world is, how darn difficult everything seemed, or how long it took me to do things, but I didn't. I was too busy just loving my freedom. Each time I came across something that challenged me, instead of feeling sorrow I simply reminded myself how far I'd come. Heck, I even signed up to the dating app called Blendr and had some fun and frolics with total strangers. I remember

Mama Renke popping over to visit – or, shall I say, to do a mother's snoop. With a condom in her hand, she yelled from my bedroom: 'Samantha, what's this?'

I was mortified and bewildered as I thought I had got rid of the bloody thing.

'What does it look like?' I replied proudly.

'Get rid of it,' was all she could manage and that was the end of an awkward conversation. It was enough, however, to confirm that things wouldn't, couldn't return to how they once were.

My sister even moved out and I was left to manage a home all by myself. Pottering around literally became my favourite pastime. I was a woman possessed. I had my own ribbon drawer and even buying my own toilet paper was liberating. I was smitten with my new-found independence. But I was still miserable AF at work. This sounds awful to say, but as I looked around the staffroom – at the teachers who had been there for decades – I felt trapped. I saw my future in them, and I didn't want it.

The appeal of how people perceived me – smashing those negative stereotypes – started to waver. I started to realise that living for other people was like a sugar rush. Great at the time, but when you crashed you were left hollow.

I slipped into a deep depression. I hadn't felt this way since my time at college, but I felt there was no place for me to share my sorrow. I had told Mama Renke to leave me alone and I had a four-bedroom bungalow to myself. Hadn't I got all I wanted? Surely, I had no right to feel depressed? I convinced myself that my sadness was my being ungrateful, instead of my simply wanting to keep pushing and dreaming big. I think many of us feel very guilty when it comes to wanting more, particularly when we see others suffering or facing hardships greater than our own. We have to try to push these thoughts away, otherwise we'll never move forward.

It was at this time that social media began to emerge. MySpace meant you could chat to anyone and everyone, and the new kid on the block, Facebook, had everyone hooked, me included. One day, I received a friend request from an old pal. Nathan, now an out-and-proud gay man living in London, once dated my best friend, Laura, when we were teens. He used to literally live on the same street as me, a few doors down, and we'd hang out, getting up to no good in the park behind our homes after school and on weekends. We'd lost contact over the years and I was so delighted to reconnect. He was such a breath of fresh air, a singer and dancer, and always so full of life. Simply intoxicating.

We kept in touch online for months and even met up when he returned home that Christmas. We instantly became incredibly close, and I disclosed my desperation and unhappiness to him. We had such a deep connection and respect for one another. I guess this was because we both knew what it felt like to be treated differently.

To have to hide who we were in order to be accepted and not defined by a label. We spoke on the phone almost daily.

'I would do anything to live in London. You are so lucky, Nathan,' I would say.

'You should come and visit me,' he suggested.

I remember the conversation so clearly because I was angry at him for being so flippant and for not addressing the complexity behind my travelling to London. True, it isn't always as easy as one, two, three when you have a disability. The most mundane activity like hopping on a train needs to be planned with military precision, given the problems: limited wheelchair spaces, and having to hope that assistance turns up on time (or at all) to help you off the train with a ramp. But the truth of the matter was that I had set limitations in my own mind. I was scared. I still doubted my capabilities. I had been indoctrinated into thinking I couldn't. Or I shouldn't. These beliefs ran deep and popped up when least expected.

Things were just going so fast. So fast for someone who had only recently learned how to make a cup of tea. Now London? Even though I'd just made the most gigantic step by living on my own, going all the way to London felt like asking me to go to Mars.

I don't want to make light of this period of my life or the person I was back then because my fear was a byproduct of the label that society put on me. Looking at my life now and how liberated I am just a decade later makes that Samantha seem rather pathetic in comparison. I could berate myself and regret not getting the courage sooner to confront my mother or overcome all those negative labels and be wild and free much sooner, but at the time it was real. I still couldn't see how incredibly I was doing and I needed to celebrate that fact. I had spent so many years afraid and toeing the line. Now I was making waves, even if to the outside world those waves were in a paddling pool.

In many ways I was still holding on to my label. Fear took hold. But something had shifted. This fear was tinged with excitement. Thoughts of what I could do, or what I thought I could do, had shifted. Now, anything was possible. The only thing getting in my way was me.

Now, whenever I doubt myself, I grab a good old-fashioned pen and paper and I list all the incredible things I've done, the big and the small, and I read them back to myself. You soon come to realise that you are always moving forward. You are always achieving and accomplishing things, even if in the moment you feel like a failure. So, here's to Samantha ten years ago. You were simply amazing. I'm proud of you. You were exactly where you needed to be.

After Nathan's ludicrous suggestion, I ghosted him for a week or so, totally pissed off that he could not see how difficult it would be for me to visit him. I had expected more from him. Yet, each night, I dreamed I was in London.

I'm pretty shit at being a bitch and couldn't stay mad at Nathan for long. My shield softened and we resumed our normal daily conversations. This time, however, I would always ask at the end of our phone calls: 'So, Nathan, hypothetically, if I came to London, how would I get into your shower? What if my wheelchair didn't fit into your bathroom? What if I had a fracture? What if the assistance on the train didn't turn up?'

Question after question. I was airing a lifetime of worries down the phone.

Poor guy. All I can say is thank you for not giving up on me and for simply saying: 'We will deal with it when and if it happens. Just get your bum down here.'

So simple, but I'd never had anyone communicate with me in this way before. Everything I did seemed to come with strings attached and obstacles to overcome, red tape and a lot of huffing and puffing. Nathan clearly didn't see me like this. For him it was black and white, and everything in between would be resolved as and when. I guess this is the true meaning of living in the present. Finding joy in the here and now and not worrying about things that haven't happened. It is something I am still working on.

Living with brittle bones means I have to think of every eventuality and, in the end, I did have to figure out how I'd go to the loo if my wheelchair couldn't even fit through the doors. I am an overthinker and he was a free-as-a-bird fella and, somehow, we needed to meet in the middle.

Nathan's way of thinking was refreshing, and I was completely intrigued. I really wanted to emulate his way of being. So, I took a deep breath and resolved to go to London. Even the act of booking the tickets over the phone set my heart racing.

I didn't tell Mama Renke, deciding instead to slip it into the conversation a few days before my trip. The co-dependency I'd relied on for so many years lingered in my subconscious. Inside, I was worried she would say no and, considering she was the one who needed to drive me to the station, I still felt like that needy, infant-ilised Samantha around her. She didn't believe me at first – I guess she didn't think I'd make such a bold leap – but she knew Nathan and his family and, after airing her concerns and having a number of phone calls with Nathan, she seemed pleased for me. Perhaps I'd underestimated her.

In the summer of 2009, I took the train by myself to London and, for the next two years, I would spend my holidays or long weekends with Nathan, literally living my best life. Nathan showed me so many new and excit-ing things and with each trip my confidence grew. But every time I left, I felt like I was leaving behind the life I desperately wanted. Every hungover train journey back to Lancashire became harder and harder. I would sit in the train, daydreaming, and although my dreams should have reflected the wild partying and the shopping sprees, the bright lights and never-ending excitement I'd just experienced that weekend, they didn't. I simply sat and found myself imagining the same simple vision in my mind, on repeat.

In that vision, I am in my very own accessible home, no step at the door, as I roll out on to the pavement, sun almost blinding me with its light. In front of me is an accessible black cab, door wide open and ramp firmly mounted, the driver assisting me into the vehicle. Simply this, over and over. Nearly every day for almost two years, I played this in my mind. I was manifesting, just like I did as a child. No exaggerated dream, no 'best bits' of the capital, no glamour or fantasy. Simply me living as I would in London. Content. Happy. Taking pleasure in the little things. Practising gratitude and valuing the importance of autonomy.

Finding a wheelchair-accessible home anywhere is close to impossible, yet each day I would sit curled up and cozy in my bed and frantically scroll through the London listings of apartments for rent. I would search for a ground-floor flat with a wet room, anything I could call my home. Each evening ended, however, in disappointment, not only for myself but also for others in my situation. I was left with a burning anger that things for disabled people had to be so fucking difficult and unfair. It was just another reminder that society wanted to keep me oppressed and in my place. Even if I found a half-decent property and could cough up the funds to adapt it, most landlords wouldn't allow me to do so. Adapting a home was still seen as something that could devalue a property; no one seemed to appreciate that it would actually do the opposite. After all, disabled people don't have lives, so why do we need to think about their needs?

Then, by pure chance and what I can only describe as a darn miracle, I found what I had been looking for.

It was now or never. I had a very small window to accept a flat in London. Like a month. Everything inside me felt alive. Anxiety poos galore, but my instinct knew it was right. I knew this was where my life was heading. All the worries that came with such a huge move simply didn't matter.

I'd learned from Nathan to follow your happiness and make a decision. So, I did. I chose to leave my job, my friends, my home and my family to move over 200 miles away so I could start a new and exciting chapter. It all seemed to be happening so quickly. But there was one thing I needed to do first. I told Mama Renke to sit down.

'Mum,' I said, 'I have something important to tell you.'

I'd secured a property, signed the tenancy agreement, and told a lot of people about the move. But not my mum. We were in the kitchen. As instructed, she sat down, her face pale and expressionless.

She grappled at her chest. 'Lord, you aren't pregnant, are you?'

'Nope, not pregnant. I'm moving to London!'

This period of my life taught me a great deal. It taught me to be true to myself. To live the life I wanted and not what others felt comfortable with. Moving to London was an enormous deal to me. I dreamed big and was on my way to realising those dreams.

Your dreams, will of course, be different to mine. You might want to start a business, do a degree, move to Ibiza. But whatever those dreams are, the principle is the same. You need to follow your heart and say yes to the opportunities that come along. Be bold, be brave and chase that rainbow!

5

Fake It Till You Make It

'Simply say yes!'

Samantha Renke

O kay, so you were brave and strong, you said yes. You made the decision. Hurrah, no more indecisiveness; you are the master of your own destiny about to start living your dream. Now what? Well, now the only thing you can do is fake it till you make it.

Just to be clear, I am not condoning falseness or asking you to make shit up, like proclaiming your fluency in Mandarin when the closest you've come to learning a foreign language is singing along to *Dora the Explorer* and ordering chicken chow mein at a restaurant that one time.

Nor do I want you to feel like you need to become someone you're not, like adding 'contortionist' as a special skill on your CV (although that one would be pretty cool). I am simply saying that a new chapter brings new challenges. That spark, that courage and strength you mustered up to make your life-changing choice, it all needs to stick around . . . because saying yes is just the beginning. You will need to get used to saying yes a heck of a lot if you want to make your dream a reality.

Sustaining your dream will be your biggest challenge yet. But, by golly gosh, it will be worth it, I promise!

I learned pretty quickly that the grass isn't necessarily always greener elsewhere, but that doesn't mean you can't make it grow yourself. I love the feeling of waking up the day after you've said yes to your new adventure, like you've been reborn. You feel so unburdened from your indecision. There's that excitement, that butterfly-tummy feeling, thinking about what awaits. The day after that, however, often comes with the almighty realisation of the terrifying nature of your decision.

It usually goes like this: 'Mother-chuffing crap-a-doodle, what have I just agreed to?' You're still excited, but those pesky anxiety poos are making an unpleasant reappearance. Doing what you love can often be glamorised. That's not to say it won't be fabulous and one of the best things you will do for yourself, but we are led to believe that, once we are pursuing our dreams, everything always falls into place and all will be hunky-dory. We hear inspirational and motivational stories from people living their best lives – but often what we're seeing is just an Instagram life. We witness the nice bits, the achievements, but not the zillions of bumps along the way. In reality, hard work is still hard work even if it comes from doing what you love. Bills still need to be paid, pandemics still come to bite you in your derrière and that anxiety you've battled with all your life doesn't just go away because you are going all Marie Kondo and sparking joy left right and centre. The world keeps turning, even if you are in your element.

For example, I love appearing on morning television; it's probably one of the best things I get to do. The adrenaline rush, the people you meet, the realisation that thousands of people are watching you. It's all a huge thrill. There really is nothing like it. But the super early mornings aren't fun. I barely sleep two or three hours the night before, so scared am I that I will sleep through my alarm. Then there's the aftermath. You are often whisked swiftly into a taxi after any appearance. So full of pride, giddy like a child, heart still pumping. It's always a little surreal. 'Wow, Sam, this is what you do for a living.' The feeling of accomplishment is exhilarating.

I come home to an empty flat and the silence is deafening. I'm still so wired and want to share my accomplishment with my nearest and dearest. But they are normally at work and can't take my calls, so I turn instead to social media to see how I've been received. Big mistake. You can have a million lovely interactions then you scroll and see the meme of an Oompa Loompa or the words 'midget freak'. They slice through me like butter. I sit alone and, although I know I should pop on the kettle and forget about that nasty individual, I can't. For someone with anxiety, and who has battled mental-health issues, this rollercoaster of emotions can play havoc with my mind. I can often go from feeling invincible to complete despair and loneliness in the space of a few seconds.

I also convince myself each time I make an appearance that it will be my last. That my performance wasn't good enough and I won't be invited back. I battle with imposter syndrome like you wouldn't believe. This is where I doubt my abilities and often feel like a fraud, something more prevalent among women and those who are working class. Oh, and those belonging to minority groups, like those with a disability.

I remember having a full-blown panic attack on the set of a BBC Sunday morning show. It was *Sunday Morning Live* and I was there to debate the newspaper stories of the week. Beside me was a well-known male journalist who was to accompany me during the section. We sat ready for a rehearsal run-through. I have to set up my wheelchair in the right position for the shot, so I'm always brought into the studio super early. The crew have to move the furniture out and then position everything back around me once I'm in place, so I look like I've seamlessly glided in without fuss. This means a swift exit is never an option and it is another reason why I go for a pee at least six or seven times before we go on air. Once I'm in, I am trapped with no escape.

On this particular day, the presenters begin reading the autocue, and my heart feels like it could fly out of my chest. I honestly don't think I am able to formulate words. I have done this many times before, but today all I can hear is my internal voice. *Why are you here, Sam? You can't do this. You aren't as intelligent as the others; you're going to fuck this up and look so foolish. You aren't good enough. You will disappoint everyone.*

I have experienced overwhelming thoughts before, but I'd equate them to normal, healthy nerves. This is something much more sinister, toxic and brutal. You know when you yell at a dog for chewing on the sofa and its head droops and its tail curls round and under its body? This is me.

The rehearsal ends and I am close to tears. I lock eyes with the presenter, Ria Hebden, someone I also call a friend, and without thinking I blurt it out.

'I'm having major imposter syndrome – right now!'

Saying it out loud is the best thing I can do. I guess I think that by letting everyone know what is going on in my mind I can negate any fuck-up because I can't back out now even if I want to. Everyone is so kind and knows exactly what I am feeling because they, too, have felt it time and time again.

Five, four, three, two . . .

We are live. I smile and deliver my part fluently, much less rigidly than during the run-through. I have done it with ease and, before I know it, I am being helped into a taxi on my way home.

Sometimes, then, the stress of maintaining your dream becomes a burden in itself. It's like you've found the Holy Grail. It's so precious and important that you start to put an enormous amount of pressure on yourself because the thought of losing what you've got is unbearable. This can actually stop you enjoying yourself and taking moments to celebrate what you have already accomplished. Instead, you start to live in fear.

I often hear from parents that something that once excited them, like flying or driving, now terrifies them, because once they've got children, the stakes are so high. The same applies when living your dream. We can become so worried about losing everything we've worked so hard for that we become paralysed. Or we can simply become too comfortable and stop learning or challenging ourselves.

It's okay to say that living your dream isn't always a bed of roses or to discover that the path you thought you wanted isn't where you should end up. The way I see it is like this: dreams are like stepping stones – we hop from one to another. Each stone brings its own challenges; some are slippery or so small we struggle to keep our balance. Some are wide and flat and cradle us, so that we may even be able to rest and lie in the sunshine for a moment. But each stone is important. Each has its part to play, and we need to find gratitude in them all because with each step comes wisdom and value.

Having that on-set panic attack was necessary because it made me address some deeper-rooted insecurities. As someone who has achieved many things, I know there have been times when I have been selected for opportunities simply because I tick a box. I have filled someone's quota. With diversity and inclusion on many institutions' agenda – none more so than in the world of entertainment – I was, at the beginning of my career, part of a very small pool of disabled creatives who made some headway in the industry, and, for a time, it felt like we were being dragged out to make a show or production seem more diverse. We'd then be put back in our box, never really given the opportunity to grow or learn, climb the ladder, or to make a real career out of our passion. Instead, we would get only token opportunities every few months, if that.

I've always tried to see the positive in tokenism, my philosophy being that if I can get a wheel in the door then I can make waves from the inside. But the notion that you've been hired due to one facet of your identity can be internalised and, yup, that's right, manifest when you are sitting in a studio almost eight years later and about to go live on morning television.

Having that episode made me have an open conversation with myself. I asked if doing this work still made me happy. I also challenged my own doubts. *Okay, Sam, you may have been a token at some point but to sustain what you are doing takes real passion, real skill and real courage.* I needed to have this bump in my journey to remind myself who I was and what I was capable of.

In fact, my move to London was about to launch me into the bumpiest trajectory I had ever experienced. Buckle up; we are in for one heck of a ride.

I moved to London on 20 February 2012. The date is etched into my mind. It was such a milestone for so many reasons, and each year I celebrate it as I would a birthday. I still couldn't quite fathom what I'd done. I'd always let other people dictate my next move, so taking charge of my own life seemed so unlike me. Yet in the same breath I felt for the first time like I was being true to myself. I didn't overthink it and the haste with which everything happened worked in my favour as I had no time to doubt my decisions. It was all systems go.

I moved into a partially adapted flat. By this I mean the doors were slightly wider to accommodate a wheelchair and the light switches were lower. There was a walk-in wet room and the bottom of the cupboards in the kitchen were removed so that I could in theory wheel as close as possible to the hob and sink (although the kitchen work surfaces were still far too high for me to reach; they were parallel with my eyeline). The building belonged to a housing association and was earmarked for civil servants and key workers: teachers, nurses and the odd fireperson. I bet you are hoping I'll tell you all I had a fling with a sexy fireman. Alas no, but my neighbours down the hall always gave me food when they celebrated Eid, so I guess that's a win.

The flat was on the fifth floor with one lift, which I soon learned would often be misused or, worse, vandalised. I regularly became stranded like Rapunzel in my tower. I also learned that most food delivery services don't deliver without the use of a lift in buildings more than three stories high. Luckily, I was the queen of bulk buying. I think something about growing up with not a huge amount meant that now as an adult with an income, I felt a comfort in a fully stocked fridge. Soon the flat contained so much food it looked more like a bunker designed to withstand a zombie apocalypse.

The flat also had a generously sized balcony, a real luxury, and a must in an urban setting. The only snag was that the threshold was so high I couldn't get my wheelchair over it. A weird ramp had been left behind that aimed to solve this barrier, but it was so steep and unstable that there was not a chance in hell I'd use it. This is something many disabled people are used to – accessibility features that have clearly never been designed by or tested on disabled people, which means they are often rendered unusable or even dangerous.

It's an odd feeling living in an environment that isn't designed for you. I often equate living in a disabling world with being a child standing outside a candy store – you can see all the wonders the shop has to offer but you can't get past the glass pane. There is an air of cruelty about it. At the time, I genuinely didn't care about how much more difficult my life was in a flat that wasn't fit for purpose. Nothing mattered except for the fact that I was here. I had made it; I was in London. *You've got this, Sam. I mean, how hard can it be? Remember, it wasn't that long ago you struggled to make a cup of tea and now you are in a flat in central London, ready to take on the world.*

I applaud my optimism back then, but now I see that flat for what it was. Discrimination. Disabled people are often pushed into submission; made to feel grateful for the little scraps of help we are thrown. We are often expected to feel thankful for the limited pockets of accessibility society has to offer instead of being encouraged and supported in calling out inequalities when our civil rights are being totally disregarded. We are so often faced with 'abled saviours' who like to remind us that their store has a lift or that their taxi has a ramp, as though every disabled person owes a debt of gratitude for these basic amenities.

Truth be told, my physical and mental wellbeing took a battering living in the flat. I struggled so much and would regularly experience hairline fractures from exerting myself too much. Yet I was constantly praised for my determination. You go, girl, overcome those barriers! You can't reach the hob but you managed to cook yourself a pasta dish. You nearly poured scalding water on your lap and the whole process exhausted you, but you did it. The reality is that disabled people shouldn't have to overcome anything.

For a long time, I felt as though the harsh and relent-less barriers I faced were simply sacrifices I had to make to pursue my dream – because nothing comes easy, right? I'd come to believe that my strength lay in bat-tling a disabling world. But no one should have to sacrifice their wellbeing just to have life experiences like everyone else. I see this now, but back then I was too afraid to question anything for fear of seeming ungrateful.

I lived in the flat with two other wheelchair users. This was, as we called it, our 'launch pad' – a tempor-ary home, our foot in the door, so to speak. We guessed six months tops then we'd go our separate ways. Off into the sunset singing tra, la, la, la . . . How naïve we were. Finding this flat was like finding a needle in a hay-stack, so I'm not sure why we thought we'd miraculously move to London and all three of us would subsequently find separate, accessible homes. Ignorance is bliss, I guess, or perhaps we were simply too intoxicated by this new phase in our lives. Or maybe we were in a bit of denial. I certainly felt like anything was possible at the time. We'd done something amazing, and we were riding that high.

The flat was pretty small: two bedrooms and an open-plan living/dining-kitchen space. Originally, I was to share a room with one of the other flatmates. Not ideal, but beggars can't be choosers. And it was tempor-ary, right? The flat was in a gloomy, clinical-looking block with fluorescent lights and the kind of speckled blue carpet tiles more at home in a third-rate office. The bathroom had no windows, and the handrails were cheap plastic and reminded me of hospitals. One of my real bugbears is when people think that just because a space needs to be made accessible, it can't be made beautiful too.

Before I moved in, I had everything prepared. I'd handed in my month's notice at work, I'd arranged removal vans to collect my belongings, I'd even sold most of my things on eBay so I had extra cash to see me through. The loss of my All Saints leather boots still pains me to this day, but I meant business. I was a woman on a mission and sacrifices had to be made.

The tenancy agreement and deposits and all that jazz had been finalised. I felt like a proper grown-up. You know, I hadn't even seen the flat in person before I signed. I'd been shown some photos and the other two had visited as they both lived closer than me. I trusted their judgement – a grand leap of faith – but I also followed my instincts. I knew this was the right move so I seized it with all my might.

I moved in a month later than the other two as I had to complete my work notice and, within that time, something had shifted. It was put to me that there was not enough space for me to share a room any more. I wasn't sure what to do with this information. Was I being asked to pull out? No one ever said those exact words, but I felt like I was supposed to agree and say, 'Oh well, you two have fun, I'll stay put.' I honestly couldn't believe what was happening. I had just quit my job, spent so much money on the move, and now, technically, I didn't have a place to sleep.

I'd never felt anger like this before. If anyone thought they could take this away from me they had another think coming. There had to be a practical solution. We would draw straws and the shortest straw would live in the living-kitchen space. Sod's law: I drew the shortest straw. Looking back, I still cannot believe I lived in an open-plan living-kitchen area with no privacy for over six months.

Of course, we set out some rules and guidelines which meant the other two couldn't come in and out of the kitchen whenever they wanted, but it was far from ideal and the atmosphere in the flat soon became hostile. What had started as three people championing one another went very sour very quickly. Every time I opened the front door I felt a wave of animosity, anger and sadness fill the space. Even when no one was home. It just lingered, seeping into the walls and crevices.

I was being suffocated by the negative energy. I cried myself to sleep almost every night. How could this have gone so fucking wrong? To make matters worse, I didn't tell anyone back home how desperately unhappy I was. I felt there was an unspoken pressure for me simply to give it all up and call it quits. I guess many of those back home couldn't understand why I'd given up a stable career and a lovely home with family and friends on my doorstep to live miles away like a student. But this wasn't a teenager experimenting with pot or rebelling against their parents. This was my future. I wanted to stay; I needed to stay. This wasn't about saving face. This was my dream, and I wasn't going to let anyone end it prematurely.

I was for a long time so full of hate, something I never thought I could be. I was angry at the way things had turned out. I was angry that I was living in a bloody living room. I was angry that I felt so alone and above all, I was angry at the people I lived with. At the time, I saw them as selfish – how dare they fuck with my dream?! I was so consumed by hatred that I adopted a victim mentality. The world's largest violin was on display, and I played it every day. I'm pretty sure if you asked the other two their side of the story, they would say that I could be a total bitch at times, and they'd be right. I was only seeing things from my perspective.

Now I look back and I'm actually able to smile. No heart full of hate, just so much gratitude. Yes, gratitude. I wasn't the only one with a dream. We all had one. We all moved to London to start a new chapter and to push our own boundaries. We were all scared and overwhelmed by adulthood and we were all simply trying to find our place in this world. No one's dream was more important than the others. I almost let the hatred consume me, but it was so misguided.

That feeling of injustice should have been directed elsewhere. Towards the systemic ableism that we see all around us. All three of us deserved better. We represented disabled people across the globe who are never given the chance to dream. We were three incredibly strong-willed and passionate disabled people who wanted to simply live in a home where we didn't struggle. Where we didn't have to stock up on beans and loo roll for fear the lift would break every second day. Where we could get our wheelchairs over the balcony and enjoy a glass of vino outside on a summer's day.

Although it was a really crappy situation for everyone involved, the doom and gloom triggered my fight or flight response. I was not for one moment complacent. I did not for one second take my circumstances for granted. I had said yes to my dream, but that was only the beginning of my journey. The grass clearly wasn't greener, but that didn't mean I had no room to grow.

I honestly believe that if I had been happy that first six months, I would not be sitting here writing this book. I'm grateful it wasn't all happy families, as odd as that may seem, because the animosity I felt meant I never wanted to be there. I despised it so much that I would spend as little time in the flat as possible. I pushed myself to go out, to network, to meet people. Create a presence.

Before long, London knew exactly who Samantha Renke was. I was like a cat spraying and marking her territory. I didn't feel heard or respected back at the flat, but that didn't mean I wasn't deserving of those things. I retracted into my shell at home, but this only meant I came alive when I went out. I've always loved making people smile or laugh and, yes, I enjoy being the centre of attention. This itch wasn't being scratched at the flat so, when I went out, I was hell bent on turning heads in any room I rolled into.

I partied hard and I partied good at the beginning of my London adventure, so much so the first three years are pretty much a blur. A magical blur. I had a lot of adolescence to make up for. Now 26, I felt like I was reliving my youth. Soho became my hunting ground and the LGBTQ+ community took me in with the most enormous, loving and completely embracing arms. I felt like everybody's little sister. It didn't matter that I was disabled or straight. I was a mini-mini-Kylie Minogue on wheels, and everyone seemed to love that.

My uniqueness attracted a lot of attention, most of it good, some of it unwanted. In the saturation of people that is London it can be hard to stand out. But I did. Little Samantha Renke, not one to succeed, written off as a baby, no boyfriend, small-town Lancashire lass. But in London – at least among the LGBTQ+ community – I had notoriety.

It was exhilarating. I was in my element, all eyes on me, but in the best way, not the sneers or wide-eyed stares of ignorance. This time I was being looked at with adoration, playful curiosity and lust. I wasn't the girl in the wheelchair from Leyland. I was the off-the-wall, spontaneous, sassy, courageous and daring Samantha who had quit her job and moved over 200 miles from her family and friends to live her dream.

I remember on one occasion sitting in a club in Leicester Square, chatting to a young guy who was miserable at work.

'Just leave, you can do it!' I yelled at him over the music. 'If I can do it, so can you.'

There I was in a nightclub acting as a life coach to strangers. I loved being heard, being a role model, a support to others, and I also loved how my confidence grew and grew with each encounter. London is known for its eccentricity, its come-as-you-are attitude. It's a place where the misunderstood come to blossom. I revelled in my own freedom of expression. My flair for fashion also grew and I felt liberated as a woman to be as adventurous and as sexual as I chose.

I always looked on point. I'd rock up to The Box in Soho, known for its outlandish burlesque shows, seeing it as an opportunity for me to dress up in leather outfits, gimp masks, face cages or corsets, carrying a whip. Sexy, provocative, blonde hair, tits perked and ruby red lips. I always wore the biggest of false eyelashes with spare glue tucked in my purse because a girl should never leave home without glue!

I'd always head up to the private room at the top of the building but, without a lift, I would be hoisted over the shoulder of a bouncer who'd carry me all the way to the top. I often felt like a shiny new toy. Remember when you were in primary school and you collected things like stickers, Pogs or Spice Girl postcards? Well, I felt like I had a shiny sticker, and everyone would crowd around me in awe. Not patronising, just genuinely interested in who I was.

Some people loved the attention I brought, which also put them at the centre of an overcrowded dancefloor. Some took on a big brother role and some sat with me next to the speaker and smoke machines as we talked about philosophy. Everyone had a story, and I was a good listener. Capricorn through and through. For some, meeting a person with a disability was a whole new experience, especially one who was straddling a six-foot-tall Adonis with a cigarette in one hand and a vodka in the other. I think my presence meant a lot to so many people, people who didn't necessarily feel comfortable in their own skin.

I was still incredibly close to Nathan and he always made sure I was involved and included with all his fun and frolics. I also started to make friends of my own. I would be invited from one party or social gathering to another and I'd say yes to them all. The Samantha from just three years ago seemed unrecognisable. It was like I had grown up in the space of these three years. It was remarkable. I was pretty darn proud of myself, but I was once again putting myself into another protective bubble. The party bubble.

The party bubble is escapism; it's *Alice in Wonderland*. But all good things must come to an end – in the harsh light of day, with lipstick smeared and one eyelash down, receiving strange looks from passers-by who can't get past their own ignorance and who are shocked to see a small person in a wheelchair, drunk, cigarette in hand, surrounded by gay men all piling into a taxi. You still return to who you were before you stepped into that bar or nightclub.

In any case, it wasn't all party central. At the time, I was frantically applying for jobs, my bank balance dwindling with each passing week. I'd have to travel by expensive cabs to get to interviews, as public transport isn't an option for me and many Underground stations are completely inaccessible.

The blatant discrimination I faced when applying for jobs in London was like nothing I'd ever encountered back home. Once, I went across London only to find the lift in the building my interview was being held in was out of service so I couldn't even attend. The receptionist was blank, not sure what to say.

I faced knockback after knockback. Many potential employers were clearly taken aback by my wheelchair.

We don't have a disabled toilet. We won't be able to provide support! I could practically read their minds: 'If we employ her, how much money will that set us back?' The problem is that discrimination is so easy to hide and rarely gets challenged. 'I'm sorry, Ms Renke, there were many strong candidates. Unfortunately, we've gone in a different direction.'

I kept my spirits up and volunteered at a children's charity, gaining knowledge and experience three days a week. I had some savings, but they didn't last long. My core group of friends at this time all had high-flying jobs, mostly in the pharmaceuticals industry, and would often invite me to lunch in Mayfair. I obliged because I didn't want to be alone, but the lavish lifestyle couldn't be supported much longer.

My friends were incredibly sympathetic and, as things got more desperate, they would all chip in and pay for my food or drinks, but this didn't sit right with me. I was faced with the looming prospect that my London dream might have to come to an end.

The group of friends I had at the beginning of my London journey were simply incredible. I think they loved my tenacity and could see that my place was in the capital. Cristina, who is a force of nature, a badass boss bitch, got me some work taking calls for a clinical trial for lupus. I had no fucking clue what lupus was, but I said yes. I would have to call the USA (the time difference was a bitch) and talk with medical professionals and patients on a blind trail. I was so grateful for the income but, by gosh, was it dull, not to mention that no one could understand my Lancashire accent. But I knew I'd make it work somehow, even if I had to go back into teaching. Luckily for me, I didn't have to return to a life I so desperately wanted to move away from. I didn't know, but one of the parties I went to changed everything.

I'm not sure where you stand on the whole fate thing? I think some things in life happen just perfectly. One Friday I am out with Nathan when he tells me we have been invited over by his close friends, Max and Eduardo, who have just bought a huge flat right next to the Olympic stadium. It is a housewarming party, the only snag being that they are on the fifth floor and the lift has been out of action for hours. Never mind, another time.

We have almost forgotten about the whole housewarming until we receive a text – *lift is working!* The party is in full swing by the time we arrive. Pink lights, a DJ in one corner, glimpses of party decorations flickering through the crowds. There must be at least 40 people crammed in the flat. I look around; not only am I the only one in a wheelchair, but I am also the only female. I flutter my feathers like a proud peacock.

Eduardo and Max are literally the most adorable couple and welcome me into their gay bosoms. Ed and I hit it off straight away, an instant love that is as strong now as it was ten years ago. He's a chemical engineer, so intelligent and wise. Max is a quirky, slightly aloof character who happens to be a TV producer and director. In fact, almost everyone at the party has some kind of connection with film or television. I am in my element. And with this I will not disclose anything more about what happened that night and the following day. What happened in Hackney Wick stays in Hackney Wick. Perhaps when I become a millionairess and don't have to worry about my career ending I will do a tell-all, but for now, all I can say is that it was one of the best times of my life and with some of the best people I know. And it was at this party I met Max!

I remember Max would constantly come out with very random and bizarre questions.

'So, being disabled, do you get away with murder because people don't expect you to be a bad person?'

His questions always made me chuckle, but they came from a very real place of having observed my interactions over several weeks and months. I tried not to come across as a mass manipulator.

'Well, obviously I would never take advantage of people, but yes, as a disabled person, I am often infantilised or not expected to behave in certain ways. So, I suppose if people are so ignorant that they choose to see me as a label, not as an individual, then yes, I could get away with murder!'

Max invited me to have a very informal casting. He explained that he had an idea for a short indie production and wanted to see me on camera. I'd always loved drama at school and had attended a number of after-school clubs for acting. One of the groups had a scout from London visiting to cast for *Oliver!* Everyone was excited and I remember all the kids in the class sorting out their portfolios. My acting teacher pulled me over and said rather ruthlessly, but completely accurately for the time and era: 'People like you won't get cast!' At 15, this was enough to make me quit acting and never return until this chance meeting with quirky Max and his rather off-the-wall ideas.

When I arrived for the audition, the camera was all set up. Max's flatmate and editor, Lorenzo, was there to assist. Eduardo sat sipping a vodka on the sofa, as though preparing to watch a movie. In front of me was an open suitcase. Wads of money and fake drug paraphernalia littered the case. My first lesson in films – how to make fake drugs from random things you find in your kitchen cupboard.

'Okay, Sam,' said Max, 'so you've come to a drug dealer's home. He has a phone call and leaves you alone with this open suitcase full of goodies. What do you do? Action!'

Without hesitation, I grabbed as much of the contents as I could, stuffing money and little bags of flour and mints into my bra and down my knickers. Everyone was in stitches. I was always wonderfully comedic and expressive in improvisation. My reaction caught them all off guard and the cheeky, no-fucks-given character called Alice Gardner was born.

We spent the next few weeks developing a script, coming up with most outlandish situations our protagonist could find herself in and constantly thinking about how disabled people are undermined and pushed out of everyday life. This character, Alice, was essentially my alter ego, the person I sometimes wished I was. She enabled me to release some of the anger I felt at times at being disabled. At those times when I was treated like a child and disrespected.

The story of Alice Gardner mirrored some of my own life. She lived at home with her overbearing and religious mother, an exaggeration of my own circumstances. But, like me, Alice wanted more out of life; she felt stifled, so she moved to London to live with her best friend. Drumroll please ... Nathan, who ended up playing the role of my best friend.

Alice starts to swindle everyone she encounters, relieving them of their wallets and turning up to parties with wads of paraphernalia that had clearly been swiped. The character was unlucky in love and she struggled on the dating scene, not to mention that most of her friends were gay men, which meant at the end of the night she would often be left tidying up the destruction from the various parties.

One day, Alice decides to call upon a sex worker, and the story of a young woman trying to navigate a world she doesn't feel she belongs in turns into a story about unconventional friendships, with Alice and her escort finding out they have more things in common than they thought. The story was so powerful and we felt we had something magical. What started out as a quirky idea for a short indie turned into a feature film. With that, *Little Devil* was born. We all worked tirelessly on zero budget, but everyone involved knew this was a project that had to be made, even if it never went anywhere.

There was so much laughter on set, with Max often filming in his and Ed's flat. *This is it*, I thought, *this is why I came to London.* I had been in town barely a year and I'd made my first film. I was on cloud nine. We submitted our creation to a number of festivals and pitched the idea and character of Alice to several broadcasters. We were all convinced Alice and her sexy, sassy confidence needed to be turned into a series.

Meeting after meeting, unsuccessful applications, and a growing sense of disappointment ... until we received the wonderful news that *Little Devil* had been awarded Best Film at the Los Angeles Diversity Film Festival. What's more, I had been awarded Best Actress!

'This is it! This is my big break.'

I was sure I would be flooded with offers, but they never came. I was battling an industry that did not see the worth of disabled people or the need to represent them. I was battling an industry that chose only to depict disabled people as objects of inspiration at the

Paralympics or objects of pity on shows like *Children in Need*.

There was no place on television for a visibly disabled woman who loves sex, dresses stylishly and is actually a bit of a cunt. Broadcasters didn't want to take a chance – they simply weren't brave enough. More importantly, they clearly weren't listening to disabled people because the disability community was craving, *shouting* from the rooftops for a character like Alice Gardner to appear on our screens. And it's not just disabled people calling out this lack of representation; in 2020, Ofcom found that disabled people are underrepresented at all organisational levels, making up just 7 per cent of television employees overall.

The next 12 months were incredibly hard for me. I felt like I was taking on an industry that didn't want me, regardless of the accolades or raw talent I had to offer. I slipped back into my party bubble, but this time instead of seeing it as a way of networking, I saw it as a way to hide my deep sadness and feelings of being a failure. One thing did, however, change. The flat went from three occupants to two, which meant no more fucking open-plan kitchen-living. I had my own room with a door. I should have seen that as the biggest win but having a space that I could lock myself away in was not what I needed at that time.

You're going to hear a lot about my sister, Stephanie, in this book and the reason is that she is the best person for the job of lifting you up when you are feeling the lowest you possibly can be. At the time, we'd drifted somewhat apart. She was worried I was partying too much (she was totally right but I was far too stubborn to see that she was only demonstrating genuine concern). I simply saw her as a party pooper. Because of this, I withdrew from our regular catch-ups because I didn't want to be disciplined and lectured. I cut myself off from those I needed the most, looking constantly for any way to escape reality.

I wish I could tell you more about this time, but I literally can't remember much. I slept an awful lot and I drank a lot. I started to chain smoke and felt angry much of the time. I was pretty pissed off at the world and everyone in it. How could I go from winning an award to eating Pot Noodles and barely leaving my flat?

At the time it all seemed so unfair. I was convinced that this one achievement meant I could sit back and the rest would fall in my lap. Oscars, Golden Globes, the whole shebang. This was the life lesson I found the hardest. I wasn't humble or grateful any more. I had become complacent and a little self-righteous.

I've always prided myself in my self-belief and sense of worth, but the truth was I had let everything go to my head and I wasn't actually a very nice person at the time. I'd returned to a victim mentality and would throw my toys out of my pram when things didn't go my way. Do I look back and feel ashamed of the person

I'd become? No, I was learning, and I guess I'd never had this kind of success before. What had manifested inside me was a person who wanted to yell and scream, 'How dare you doubt me? I will never let that happen again!'

I was bloody fuming. I felt a lot of anger and sadness because I saw how much potential I had and how much I could grow if only there were more people like Max in the world, who saw the beauty in my uniqueness. I was his muse. I was beginning to see how much richer and happier my world could be if others simply stopped being so ignorant. I was done with jumping through hoops. I was done with being applauded for 'overcoming' systemic ableist barriers as though I should feel pride in getting one over on the system.

By being part of *Little Devil* I'd shown that disabled people can be whatever they goddamn well want, but now I felt it was up to the rest of the world to change how they saw us. I was done educating people. I saw what could be achieved so why wasn't the world listening? This attitude at its core was, I suppose, admirable. Unfortunately, my stance only hindered my own growth and in doing so I became a little bitter and almost sabotaged my own dream.

I could not rest on my laurels, and taking a stance that required the world to wake up and become more inclusive just because it should wasn't going to get me very far with my career. People needed to be educated and needed to see and listen to people like me tell them what they were doing wrong. I just didn't want that person to actually be me. I didn't want to be the guinea pig, the trailblazer or the game-changer – I just wanted to crack on with my acting career and leave all that advocacy and activism to another disabled person.

Safe to say I became incredibly bored waiting around for the entertainment industry to see the value in disabled people. But at the time I was adamant I would wait for them to buck up their ideas. I was featuring in my own Western, tumbleweed floating by, accompanied by the eerie sound of nothingness. I also felt an overwhelming sense of embarrassment. I had gone from bragging about my accomplishments to then having month upon month of nothing. The depression came back, and it hit me hard.

There was only one thing I could do in this moment of despair and that was to reach out to my sister. She could hear the desperation in my voice, the longing to succeed. I was being so hard on myself.

'I'm a failure,' I told her. 'How embarrassing!'

'You are not at all, Samantha,' she would reply. 'Listen, do you want my advice?' she added in her no-fuss, no-stress, calming tone. 'If you do one thing each day towards your goal – no matter how big or small – you will achieve your dreams.'

Slow progress is better than no progress. Something about building Rome springs to mind. I get it, though;

slow progress can be frustrating. You start to compare yourself to others and everyone seems to be doing things better, faster, with more success.

We are often encouraged to dream big. We aspire to be like those at the top: footballers, entrepreneurs, the Greta Thunbergs of the world, but if we constantly measure our accomplishments against these astronomical standards we ultimately set ourselves up for heartache and unhappiness or, like me, brutal self-judgement. Because most of us won't reach these heights and that's okay, because our own contributions to this world will be on a smaller scale, perhaps within our community or in our immediate circle: our friends and families, local charities and places of work. It's so important that we take note of our achievements, even the little ones. We need to praise ourselves for our contributions, however small, and give ourselves credit for not giving up.

Stephanie's advice was invaluable. Even on the days I felt my lowest, those self-loathing days when you literally get out of bed just to pee. Do one thing that you can say has taken you just that tiny bit closer to where you want to be. Set up a Twitter account and start to follow people you can network with. Send an email introducing yourself to the organisation you want to partner with. Find out how to set up an Etsy store or get on Eventbrite and see what's going on in your local area. YouTube the shit out of TED Talks so you know how to navigate public speaking. Get creative and design some business cards – heck, even make a list of company names you like the sound of. Or, like me, one of the first things you could do is to write a column.

I did just that and emailed it to a leading disability magazine, asking them if they would publish it. They did and I have now been a resident columnist for *Pos-Ability* magazine for over six years. That happened because I sat in my bed and wrote 500 words and was brave enough to email the editor.

Success doesn't come overnight, so instead of beating yourself around the head about what you haven't got or what you aren't doing, stop and take a deep breath. Unburden yourself from the pressures of constantly having to go-go-go to be successful. Take a tip from me and my sister and simply do one thing, no matter how big or small each day, and you will get to where you want to be.

6

Be Your Own Muse

*'I am my own muse. I am the subject
I know best. The subject I want
to know better.'*

Oroma Elewa

If I could go back to my younger self, I'd simply say this: spend less time worrying about trying to fit in, trying to be popular, a carbon copy of someone else. Stop looking to others for validation and inspiration. Instead, invest more time in yourself and become the person you'd be proud of, inspired by and thankful for. Be your own goddamn muse. Forget about finding yourself and concentrate on *creating* yourself.

I'm not disputing the importance of role models, people you look up to and feel inspired by. Heck, I'd say that I aspire to be one of those people and, by gosh, as a disabled kid I longed for the day I could turn on my television screen or open the pages of *Mizz* and *Girl Talk* (popular nineties magazines, in case you were wondering) and see people who looked like me.

One of the reasons I agreed to write this book was simply in the hope I can be of comfort to others. I hope my words make people feel heard, less isolated and, yes, although I have a complex relationship with the word (which we will come on to very soon), I am going to say

I hope to be an inspiration to others. But wouldn't it be nice if we all spent just that little bit more time learning who we are instead of always looking to others for answers?

The best thing you can ever do is invest in yourself. Own it. Own your identity. Your uniqueness. Your insecurities. Your strengths. Recognise that what you bring is wonderful and you can find an inner peace and a sense of worth in a world that can at times seem like it's spiralling out of control. You know when people say, 'You come into this world alone and you leave this world alone'? That's all sounds rather morbid and sad, as though there's no real point to it all. No real point in falling in love or making connections with others. What I hear is actually rather the opposite. I see this as an opportunity to celebrate yourself, to fall in love with you, and to make the biggest connection of all. With your own self.

This, I believe, has always been my biggest strength, perhaps because I spent a lot of my childhood alone. Either in hospital or in my bedroom. As a child who could fracture her bones with a sneeze, the outside world was a daunting place, which meant I spent a lot of time in my own company. I believe I was 14 by the time I had my first sleepover at a school friend's. Even that took some persuasion as many of my friends' parents didn't want the responsibility of having a brittle-boned kid under their care.

True, I didn't have as many playdates or social inter-actions as most other kids growing up, but this allowed me to get to know myself from an early age. It allowed my imagination to run wild and gave me the ability to find peace and a sense of solitude in my own dreams and my own company. My innate sense of understanding who I am has always been a great comfort in times of complete chaos and trauma. Whenever I had a bone fracture, I'd give myself a pep talk: *you've got this Sam!* It allowed me to stay cool, calm and collected until the ambulance arrived and then to articulate my needs, how I should be lifted without causing more distress, and what medication I needed.

I have always held myself in the highest regard. That isn't as wanky as it sounds. Whenever I'm asked during an interview who I am inspired by, who's my muse, I will without hesitation say that it's me! This isn't because I don't think other people can teach me some-thing or I can't be blown away by people's talents, but the reality is I really didn't have any role models for a long time. What I've always had is an unwavering belief in myself. You shouldn't feel embarrassed or modest about saying that you admire your own strengths or the fact that it was you and only you who got yourself through some really shitty experiences. Because for me, true confidence is not entering a room thinking you are superior to everyone else, it's feeling that you don't have to compare yourself to everyone else there.

I've been called narcissistic, cheeky, loud, full of myself and egotistical. I've even had someone think I'm drunk because of my 'overly chatty' behaviour. All of which says to me that people aren't ready for a successful and confident disabled woman.

My confidence and self-belief as a youngster didn't go unnoticed either. I was often seen as too opinionated, arrogant and cocky. I remember my primary school teacher yelling at me: 'I think you've said enough for one day, don't you, Samantha?' Some of the boys in my class had been handing around a book on biology with naked pictures, sniggering and shouting 'boobies!' at the girls. I took it upon myself to tell my teacher to remove the book. I was mortified by her response as, deep down, I was a people-pleaser and hated getting into trouble. But I always prided myself on being able to communicate and owning my confidence.

Unfortunately, self-belief can intimidate others, even if you are a child. I needed to be this confident, perhaps sometimes cocky youngster, because I needed above all to believe in myself. Being a kid with a disability was hard but being an adult with a disability is exhausting and isolating and scary. Putting myself on a huge pedestal is not only good for my soul, it also allows me to know what I'm capable of and to dip into my inner strength whenever I need to. It is my biggest weapon, one that prevents me from drowning in a world that keeps taking away my life raft.

Once you start to believe in yourself, the rest simply falls into place. Your confidence exudes from you, and confidence is powerful. It is intoxicating and contagious. Confidence looks and feels beautiful, not only to you but to those around you. It radiates from within and, like a perfectly formed poached-egg yolk, it spills out, leaving its bright, rich imprint all around. Or, if we are sticking with this little metaphor, it trickles into your baked beans and hash browns. I'm totally starving as I write this part – can you tell?! It's a good thing I normally eat before I sit down to write or else this book would be jam-packed with random food analogies.

I bet you are all thinking, yes, cheers for that, Samantha, all sounds lovely but easier said than done. I absolutely agree. It's hard work to feel like you are amazeballs and radiate confidence, especially when the world – even those closest to you – doesn't see it or, worse, tries to stifle it and gaslight you. Or when social media tells you that you should constantly look to others to feel alive. Or when you encounter people who tell you that you aren't special or that your uniqueness is a bad thing.

Boy, do I get it. As a disabled woman, I'm repeatedly told I'm ugly, undesirable, unintelligent, not worth the time of day and not worth investing in. I've lost count of the times I've had someone tell me that if they had a disability they would rather die. I shit you not, this is an actual thing people say, regularly, to disabled people.

I mean, as a disabled person what am I supposed to do with that statement? For me, it normally hits like a ton of bricks, a disgusting reminder of how society still depicts disability as something to be ashamed of or sees it as a lesser life. My kneejerk reaction would be to reply: 'Well, thank God I don't look like you because if I did I'd want to kill myself' – but that would be my ego talking and would not help anyone.

Instead I reply by saying: 'I have an amazing, rich, exuberant life and I bloody love who I am!'

Okay, so perhaps I don't use as many adjectives, but you catch my drift.

What can I say? It's hard, especially when you are constantly told you aren't good enough. You are too fat, too black, too gay, too disabled. It's a challenge to find that inner strength each day to say 'I am enough' – actually, I am more than enough, I am all that I need to be and everything else in my life is a beautiful bonus for which I'm grateful. It doesn't come naturally. This inner power and strength may not be with you most days, but if you can learn to believe that you can rely on yourself and be proud of who you are, you will find that other people's negative actions and words have little or no bearing on your own happiness.

My middle niece, Marcia, is literally everything I want everyone to be and more. We attended her sister Isla's cheerleading championship, the sports hall awash with hundreds of kids and their families from different teams. All the contestants were touching up each other's make-up and hair and taking selfies. Even the kids who weren't competing all looked like their siblings: same clothes, same hairdos. Then, in walks Marcia in unicorn leggings, glittery unicorn sweater, unicorn headband and unicorn handbag. Nothing matched, she was all the colours of the rainbow – there was absolutely no worry we'd lose her in the crowd. She walked into that hall with her peers all staring at her and she owned everything about herself. I couldn't keep my eyes off her and thought to myself that, in a sea of sheep, she was absolutely a beautiful unicorn.

We all need to be a bit more Marcia. Why be a sheep when you can be a mother-chuffing unicorn?

If, like me, you have gone through most of your life with other people underestimating you, tearing you down instead of building you up, do what I do: shift your perception, change how you see your circumstances. Be your own muse and realise that you can change your narrative. This is exactly what I did as a young girl. I came to the realisation that when no one expects that much from you, they are giving you a gift. Carte blanche.

You are given the freedom to be whatever you want and to do anything you choose with your life. This epiphany, let's call it, came to me after a rather traumatic event and, although it brought a lot of sadness, it also allowed me to understand the power of believing in myself and to create a person proud of her identity. Disability and all.

I attended my local primary school, Leyland Methodist. It was quaint and had a quirky head teacher, Mr Graham, who named his guitar Brownie. We'd be tortured each morning having to listen to Simon and Garfunkel's 'Bridge Over Troubled Water' as we lined up for assembly. One of our teachers made us sing 'I must, I must increase my bust' while waving our arms back and forth as a mini morning workout. So, you know, just a regular school that smelled of sun and sweaty feet.

At the time, we lived literally five minutes round the corner.

Each morning I'd collect Laura, my best friend, and my mum would push me in my manual chair to the school entrance, where she'd pass me over to my teaching assistant, who'd transfer me into my electric wheelchair. You see, back then this was my only mode of getting around independently apart from bum shuffling, which the school didn't go for except now and again during PE when the whole class would have bum-shuffling races. My team always won. Naturally.

I loved my electric wheelchair. It was Ferrari red, and the seat was covered in what can only be described as dark brown ultra-fluffy sheepskin. It literally looked like Snoop Dogg had pimped my wheelchair. Chairs like these cost the earth; my current powerchair cost close to £10,000, so Lord knows how much they cost way back then.

My father's firm had come together and fundraised to buy it. The whole event even made the local newspaper, my first glimpse into 'celebrity', of course, and I relished every moment in the limelight. Both of my wheelchairs gave me different ways of being independent and each had their pros and cons. But at the time I loved how my powerchair allowed me to zip across the grass on the playing field and be with my friends during playtime.

Each evening, when the bell rang for home time, I'd park my powerchair in one corner of the school hall to be charged ready for the next day. On one occasion, the school was burgled over the weekend. Many of the windows were smashed, there was spray paint everywhere, and utterly despicable destruction had taken place. Now, I've already told you that I was a super child spy and rarely missed a beat. Despite the adults trying to protect me from this knowledge, I found out that my wheelchair had fallen victim to the vandals. Not stolen but spray-painted and, worse, the intruders had urinated and defecated on the chair. Yes, you heard that right. What disgusting scum could do that to a child's wheelchair?

In that moment I learned a few important things about life. That being disabled doesn't shield you from the anger, violence and injustices of the world. And that not everyone wants to care for and support disabled people – a stark contrast to the kindness of the fundraisers who'd raised the money for the powerchair just a few months prior. It also made me feel afraid for the first time ever. It made me believe that disability is something to be mocked. I believe this was the first time I internalised ableism.

Amid all this sadness and negativity, however, I also found inner strength. Some may say I hardened my shell and that my innocence was tarnished. I'd agree, but in that moment the harshness of the world made me determined to be strong. Deep down, I wanted to show those bullies that I would surpass them all. I hope they turn on their televisions and see my beautiful face staring back at them.

This was unfortunately the first of many occasions over the years when my sense of worth really took a beating. Cumulatively, these incidents pushed me further and further away from loving who I was and feeling pride in my identity. Pride in one's disability is complex and an idea I have still not fully unpacked. How can you have pride in a body that repeatedly lets you down? How can you have pride in a word that kinda implies you aren't capable? How can you feel pride in something many people avoid?

I have no desire to speak for every disabled person. How does that line go? If you've met one disabled person, you've met one disabled person. I can only tell you how I feel and what I have learned from the experiences I have had as a full-time wheelchair user with brittle bones.

I guess there are a few things that need to be ironed out here. First, I am a firm believer that the word 'disabled' has power and that power lies in owning its meaning and its history, and using it to push a cultural shift which sees disabled people as fucking human beings – not burdens, drains on society, unlovable or unsuccessful second-class citizens.

So, yes, I say I am a proud, disabled woman, and 'disability' isn't a dirty word. I want everyone to feel comfortable in saying the word because if you feel uncomfortable as a non-disabled person then your discomfort is a small price to pay. Let's face it, it pales into insignificance when we compare it to the constant marginalisation, oppression and discrimination of the disability community.

The way I see it – and the way many other disabled people see it too – is that we are only disabled by systemic barriers, by negative attitudes and outdated and harmful social constructs. So, if we shy away from the word 'disabled' then we are effectively turning a blind eye to systemic ableism. We do nothing to create an equal and inclusive society in which disabled people have a voice and rights.

I only became aware of this way of seeing things once I'd moved to London. I cannot express how liberating it was suddenly to see the world like never before. I'd been told from birth I was a problem, something to be fixed, and all the barriers I faced along the way were my problems to overcome. And when I did, I was praised for being strong and brave. Now I see the world so clearly. I now know that I'm not a problem at all. I never was. Now I know my uniqueness is beautiful. I now see other people's ignorance towards me as their burden to carry. Not mine. I am a unicorn not a sheep and that feels good.

I also have pride in my disability because why shouldn't I feel happy and comfortable in my own skin, in a part of me that just is? I was born with my disability. I've never known life without it. Just as I am white and female and heterosexual, my disability is simply another layer of my identity.

This is why I have a rather large bee in my bonnet about the word 'inspiration' or being called *inspirational*. You'll have to bear with me on this one because I may come across as a bit of a twat, especially if you've picked up this book in the aisle marked 'Inspirational Stories' or 'Motivational Books'. Disabled people are often never allowed to simply be individuals. We are often only viewed by our diagnosis, our medical label, or the label given to us by society. We are never allowed to express our individual identities. Why can't Bob just be Bob or Sam just be Sam?

With disability, you are either the hero or the victim. The inspiration or the burden. Nothing in between. Not real humans, just inflated caricatures of how society wants disabled people to be seen. This can impact on you in a massive way and you can lose your own identity in the mix.

I have certainly been lost down this rabbit hole myself. But identifying these tropes and understanding these labels was another step towards me regaining my own identity, feeling empowered, and understanding and embracing the beauty of my uniqueness. While unapologetically taking up space as a disabled woman in spaces that aren't made for me.

As far back as I can remember, strangers would approach me and call me inspirational. I didn't necessarily dislike the attention, but I did always find it rather odd. I used to chuckle to myself: 'You don't actually know me, I might be a horrible person, I might kick puppies in the street.' Just to clarify, I do not kick puppies in the street.

It was only when I became more active in my role as disability campaigner that I came across a TED Talk written by the incredible Stella Young. Sadly no longer with us, Stella was an incredible trailblazer living in Australia who also happened to have brittle bones. Stella spoke on a subject she called 'inspiration porn', a term she had coined to describe how disabled people are often objectified, mostly by harmful stereotypes created by the media in order to make non-disabled people feel good about themselves.

The assumption is that disabled lives are lesser and therefore any hint of success or living a 'normal' existence must be exceptional. I've had fantastic comments like, 'You dress really well, considering' or 'It's great to see folk like you out and about', as though disabled people aren't supposed to leave their parents' homes, get jobs or marry. And, if we do, we aren't supposed to look attractive or take pride in our appearance.

We see inspiration porn everywhere, especially on social media. I'm sure we have all liked a post or shared inspiration porn ourselves because we've seen, perhaps, a young disabled kid with limb difference who is a ballerina and we've felt inspired because we cannot fathom how they are dancing with no arms. The truth is I want everyone reading this book to be inspired in one way or another, but I don't want that inspiration to come from a place of comparison or for you to think that my success is something to be admired simply because I've had it tough.

I want to inspire people to be their own fucking muse and, if they find disabled people inspiring, I want them to do so because they acknowledge our lives are more difficult. Rather than using empty phrases like 'you inspire me', I want them to become our allies and advocates and call out the barriers we face instead of taking the easy route out by giving us a back-handed compliment and not doing anything to better our situation.

To this end, whenever anyone tells me I inspire them nowadays, I gracefully accept their comment, smile, and simply say: 'Thank you, what have I inspired you to do?'

I'd be a liar if I said that I've always had this comfortable relationship with my disability identity. True, I've always loved my uniqueness, but that doesn't mean I liked other disabled people. In fact, I spent most of my youth and even early adulthood trying to distance myself from other disabled people. I rarely interacted with anyone who was disabled, apart from my yearly trips to see my specialist, where I'd always run into other brittle bone kids, and the times I saw my cousin, Georgina, who was born with Down's syndrome and has other neurological conditions.

We weren't super close. I was incredibly brittle as a child, much more so than I am now, while Georgina was strong. There was only a six-month age difference between us, but we were polar opposites. She tried to grab me on the odd occasion and once succeeded in cracking me on the head with a beer. This meant my parents were always on edge when we visited my aunt and uncle's house. I laugh now because we'd have to literally build a human wall between us. I mean, I don't blame George – she wanted to play and I did resemble a tiny doll.

I went to mainstream schools, by which I mean I was the only disabled kid in the building for most of my education. Then the internalised ableism kicked in, full force, once puberty hit. Every time I thought about disability, my mind would go to those stereotypical images. I wasn't like 'them'. In retrospect I was being prejudiced to the people who in many ways I could relate to the most. I was being ableist and I wasn't even aware of it. I suppose I should feel ashamed of the way I once was but, in all honesty, I just feel sad. I also see how insidious and ingrained these stereotypes are, and how indoctrinated we are as a society when it comes to disability discrimination. I was simply another casualty of this.

In many ways, my own prejudice made me a much stronger and more compassionate activist in later life. I am not in a position to wave my finger at those who are ableist, or who perhaps are guilty of ableist microaggressions. We are all guilty of unconscious bias and we have all been indoctrinated over the years to behave in a way that separates one group of people from another. We can all unlearn and relearn and that is exactly what I did. I just had a little push from a stranger I met on a train.

It is 2008 or 2009 and I am once again visiting the hospital. It is years after my spinal fusion operation and everything in my life is kicking off. I'm in the full swing of my PGCE. The visit is a simple check-up, long and boring, and Mama Renke is with me for the company.

We always make our way by train but booking a return ticket can be tricky because we can never be sure when we will be free from the hospital. Now, a little fun fact: as a wheelchair user, you can only book assistance and a wheelchair space 24 hours ahead of your journey and most standard trains only have two or three designated wheelchair spaces. If they are booked, then tough shit.

It can all be a bit of a nightmare when you are coming from a specialist hospital which sees many wheelchair users visit from all over the country. It is a muggy, grey, wet day. The platform is poorly covered, and Mama Renke and I are sitting, soaking wet, clutching overpriced hot drinks. A voice springs up over the tannoy: 'The train arriving at platform eight to Manchester Piccadilly is delayed.' Literally the worst possible thing we could have heard.

We immediately rush to find a member of staff on the platform because getting on another train with a wheelchair is going to be difficult. As we approach one of the conductors, another young woman and her friend are talking to him. I immediately recognise that she, too, has brittle bones. The condition has some tell-tale features, something I've always really struggled to come to terms with, especially when you get strangers mistaking you for another person with brittle bones, insisting it was you they met five years ago in Benidorm and not taking no for an answer.

For me, it always signifies how some non-disabled people view disabled people, particularly if they are short and in a wheelchair, once again stripping us of our identity.

As someone who has been on TV, I receive messages weekly from other individuals who have the same condition and who have been mistaken for me. I can only imagine how irritating that must be and I always apologise. Equally, I've always been perhaps a little annoyed when someone takes credit for my hard work and accomplishments or, worse, when I am mistaken for someone who isn't a nice person. I've had a number of men insist they have seen me on an adult site. I've never seen who they have compared me to, but I can guarantee that we look nothing alike except perhaps for having the same hair colour and short stature. Whenever this happens, I often simply question them, 'What exactly do you see when you look at us?'

But there was a clear distinction between me and this rather eccentric, almost punk-rocker chick. She had dark bobbed hair, long nails, ruby-red lips with piercings and fishnet tights. We both plead our case.

'We need to get home, please help us!'

I have a Christmas works do to attend and am not about to miss out (at the time I was still working in the school and had a huge crush on the sexy French teaching assistant).

The two of us are harassing the conductor, wearing him down until we both end up in a carriage that isn't supposed to have anyone in, the half-way space with a toilet and a through passage. We sit facing one another, our gaze meeting. We exchange smiles.

'Have you been to the hospital?' I ask, not one for awkward silences. I am curious to see who this badass babe is. I've never met anyone disabled with such a flair for fashion before. She clearly gives zero fucks. I'd even say that I am rather intimidated by her presence. My own stereotypes are shattered in an instant and my internalised ableism is rampant as I stare at her rather handsome companion. *Surely that's not her boyfriend?* Told you I was totally ableist and blissfully unaware of how damaging my own prejudices are. Luckily for me, once we start chatting, my mysterious train twin is about to change how I view disability for good.

'Have you ever been to one of the annual general meetings for the Brittle Bone Society?' she asks. I reply that I haven't. I knew of the BBS, a charity specifically created to support those with brittle bones and their families, and I had seen the newsletters that came through our door. I'd glance at the black-and-white pictures of the little children with the same condition as me, but we never spoke about going to one of the AGMs. Mama Renke has since confirmed why we didn't – my dad struggled with my diagnosis and being faced with a room of other similar families would have been too overwhelming for him. It's such a shame, as I can guarantee he'd have found an inner peace if he had.

'We need people like you on our board of trustees,' she continues. 'You are spunky and, like me, don't take no for an answer. That's exactly what we need. There's an opening; you should apply.'

She reaches into her oversized handbag, strategically balanced on her foot plate, and scribbles down her email address.

'Let's keep in touch!'

At this time in my life, I was all about saying yes to new opportunities. I'd been told the role would look incredible on my CV and that was enough to make me go ahead with the application. I had no idea what being a trustee entailed, I just knew that the position would last three years with an opportunity of re-election. I was to attend quarterly meetings to discuss the running of the charity.

To apply for the role I had to become a member of the charity and attend the three-day AGM, which consisted of talks from medical professionals, exhibitions from wheelchair providers, and an opportunity for members to get to know you and take a vote to decide your fate. It all sounded incredibly official, but I subsequently found out it was more fun than it looked with a whole load of incredible people with brittle bones. I was about to enter a world I had thus far done my best to avoid.

I got the role. I acted as a trustee for six years, only standing down to pursue other projects. Each year I would attend the three-day event and, with each year, I learned to love myself and my disability identity more and more. I think there is a misconception that all disabled people have everything in common and that if we're put in a room together we all instantly become the bestest of friends. Unfortunately, this isn't the case, but what I would say is that my OI family was just that. A family. We didn't see eye to eye all the time, but there was an undoubtedly strong connection among us all, a solidarity, and an unspoken sense of understanding because even though our lives looked very different, with different interests, talents and ideologies, we could all have a good old laugh about the funniest ways we've broken our bones. Or share tips and tricks on how to reach things in top cupboards, or how to have a baby or drive a car, or which wheelchairs are the best.

I had found a community and, for the first time, felt I could be my authentic self. One year, I took my best friend, Laura, to the AGM, pre-warning her about what to expect because I remember my being rather overwhelmed the first time I found myself in a hotel lobby with hundreds of wheelchairs and little people. I wanted to share this experience with my best friend because this community had made me think differently about myself and had, ultimately, made me realise that I could be completely accepted by a group of people.

I think the staff at the hotel always had a pre-warning, so to speak, because they never made us feel different, even when, for example, we climbed out of our wheel-chairs and lay on the lobby floor to have a good old stretch, or when some of us would make out at the closing party. I was so happy and so myself. I saw the beauty in being different.

It was always bittersweet leaving the AGM, although many of us stayed in contact over social media and even met up throughout the year. It really did feel like you were leaving a different world, a safe, inclusive world. We didn't forget we were disabled; we just weren't made to feel like a burden, and we didn't have to fit into anyone's mould.

The year I took Laura, I remember the journey home clearly because we couldn't stop talking about the fun and frolics we'd had and I remember Laura being so grateful that I had invited her to share such a special event. On the way back, we stopped for something to eat at a Burger King. It was so busy and, as I sat at the table waiting for Laura to bring over my meal, I felt everybody's eyes on me. I had to question myself but, once back in the safety and comfort of Laura's car, we turned to one another and both said: 'Was it me or was everyone staring?'

We had both been so shielded by the warmth and safety of the AGM bubble, a space where such stares didn't happen. We both cried on the journey home.

Now, I understand that those people who live in ignorance, who pity disabled people, who do nothing to challenge their own ableism, are living a life that is, in my mind at least, so dull. A life in a captivity of their own making. Because I am here living my life, knowing my worth, being my own muse and I'm free.

One of the reasons I love how unique each and every one of us is – and this should be something we celebrate – is because our dreams are also unique. I'm sure we'd all agree that if everyone's aspirations were to do the same job or to decorate their houses in entirely the same way we'd live in a remarkably dull world.

Don't ever let anyone diminish your determination or accuse your confidence of being simply ego.

If I hadn't, from a young age, put myself on a very high pedestal and literally told myself every day *you are the best thing since sliced bread*, I don't think anyone else would have done it for me. You can love yourself and hold yourself in a high regard and still be humble. You can big yourself up and still lift others up too.

7

Love Your Body

Kintsugi: *The Japanese art of putting broken pottery pieces back together with gold, built on the idea that, in embracing flaws and imperfections, you can create an even stronger, more beautiful piece of art.*

You might not have the body you wanted but, you know what, as Mama Renke would often say: tough titties, it's the one you've got. So, you need to learn to make the most of it. Celebrate it. Heck, some day you may even learn to bloody love it, even when it can be a proper wanker at times.

My first cliché of this chapter, and the first lesson in self-love, is a proper good'un and goes like this: if people are going to stare, then give them something to stare at.

Boom! Such a bold, unapologetic and fierce statement and I firkin love it! It exudes confidence and liberation. Zero fucks given. However, it's taken years of practice for me to own it, to embrace every word. Now I live by it as much I can, although I appreciate that some days it's easier said than done. I love it because it acknowledges that you cannot control others or how they behave. Once you let go of that responsibility you are free to be you.

Let's face it, you will always come across ignorant, rude individuals or those who are so self-obsessed they can't see anything past their own noses, totally oblivious to others and their feelings. Those who project their insecurities onto you and those who are so toxic that even the spaces they inhabit leave you wanting to burn sage in those rooms for a week.

But our job is not to try to second-guess why some people act the way they do or to rationalise their way of being. Relinquishing this responsibility isn't excusing bad behaviour, especially when it makes you doubt your own worth. It is simply recognising that humans are humans: living, breathing sponges that absorb and are shaped by their environment and unique social circumstances, the good and the bad. We can't expect everyone to be on the same spiritual, emotional and educational path as our own, but what we can do is not let their actions control us.

I don't know about you, but I'm totally singing 'Let It Go' from *Frozen* in my head right now. I'm not, however, suggesting for one second that it's as easy as imagining a balloon in your hand and visualising letting it go. Or that this will miraculously make you become impermeable to the opinions and judgements of others. It takes practice and perseverance. It's not easy striking a balance between caring less about what people think about you, but also caring enough to gain the respect you deserve.

Be the role model you wanted as a child and learn to love yourself so that a stranger's stare or disrespectful, ignorant remark doesn't ruin your day, your week or year. This, I've found, is the biggest gift you can ever give yourself and it is integral to loving your body, nipple hairs, scars, curls and sticky-out belly button.

When you have a disability – particularly one that is clearly visible like mine – you get a lot of unwanted attention in the way of stares and glares. I would literally have to wear a bin bag to disguise my disability. It's an odd thing to think that I've never known life without people staring. As a kid, it was mostly followed up by an 'ah, bless', or some kind of free gift – sweets, a crusty teddy bear from a charity box, or a good old pat on the head. Kindness wrapped up in a pity bow.

As I grew older, the looks would be less patronising and more intrusive. Malicious at times. Intended to make me feel ugly. A freak. Abnormal. Different. Gosh, writing this just now has made me never want to return to a zoo or get a pet fish.

It's a strange feeling to have so much unwanted attention for simply being you. As a child, I was bewildered. At a very young age I would use the stares as a way to manipulate others. I honestly used to think, 'Well, if you are all daft enough to feel sorry for me then I will play up to it to get the free stuff.' I was a crafty little sod, but I guess this was my first experience of negating harmful societal stereotypes. If they were going to stare, I may as well get something out of it.

I already had such self-awareness, a skill that would get me to where I am today. The world was my stage, and I was the performer. I was cheeky, chatty and cute. A little blonde bob, which was often crimped or styled in pigtails, and my tiny little outfits. Such a small girl but one big personality. If people are going to stare, then give them something to stare at!

My enthusiasm for this attention reduced over the years. I began to see what the stares and glances really meant. The free treats and cooing over my cuteness faded and I simply became an object of curiosity. It chipped away at my sense of worth.

As a disabled person, you learn very early on that your body is seen by many as something to objectify. Every Tom, Dick or Harry will have an opinion, even when you didn't ask for one, and, let me tell you, it never gets any easier to digest. You simply learn to live with it and do your best to not let it impact on your world more than it should.

I never understood when people would advise me simply to brush it off. 'Just ignore them, Sam,' as though someone stopping in the street to look – eyes wide, mouth ajar, like you are some kind of extra-terrestrial, with no consideration of how that might make you feel – is something you can simply ignore. Ignoring it, not talking about it, and suppressing how it made me feel was not the coping strategy I so desperately needed. Because every stare was internalised. They made me feel inadequate. They were a little reminder that 'you aren't one of us, Samantha'. Pretending that the world wasn't unaccepting of disability was not helpful. It made me feel invalidated and powerless. I'd often look in the mirror and question: what do they see that is so bad?

Staring is very much an artform. It has many guises. There is the side glance; the blatant, unashamed peering with a slight open jaw in disbelief. The tap-your-mate-on-the-shoulder-to-have-a-quick-look stare. The glance with a giggle. The 'I know I shouldn't but I'm going to anyway' stare. The stare that is followed by a smile that totally negates any rudeness or ignorance and makes it all okay, right? Then there is the thirst for knowledge stare, usually from kids. 'Look, Mummy, why's that lady so small?' These are most usually accompanied by a finger point.

Then there is the stop-and-take-a-photo stare, which often happens in crowded areas as though the perpetrator thinks I won't notice. But I see you, I fucking see you, and it hurts.

The way I react has evolved over time and, in many respects, is totally dependent on how I feel on any given day. If I'm on my period, if I'm preoccupied, or if I'm in someone's company. Especially if I'm on a date – I worry that the stares of others will put them off ever returning for date two. I am constantly on high alert. I have to be honest and say for many years my knee-jerk rection to these people was to tell them to go fuck themselves. However, my impulsive desire to make others feel bad about their stares by saying something along the lines of 'take a picture, it will last longer' or simply flipping them the finger are far behind me.

Not because I'm a saint. Because, although giving them a taste of their own medicine for making me feel like crap may have given me a temporary rush of power, it always backfired and inevitably left me feeling bad for the rest of the day. I'm inherently a people-pleaser and this tit-for-tat playoff is out of character for me and so not good for the soul. Ergo, it gave them back the power.

More importantly, their actions only have power if I allow that to happen. In that moment I have a choice: am I going to let a stranger's ignorance ruin my day? It's a power conundrum, but once you believe that you deserve better and owe it to yourself not to let the stares affect you, it feels like a weight has been lifted and you genuinely start to not give a fuck.

Now, I make like a horse with blinkers on so it doesn't get startled. My biggest deflectors are the confidence and belief that I am, without a doubt, the best thing since sliced bread and, not to mention, pretty darn shit-hot (she says this while currently sporting greasy hair, stretchy leggings and so much underarm hair you could braid it).

My Superwoman cape, my self-love bubble, shields me from the stares and I simply don't notice them as much. I mean, for starters I literally have no time to notice them. I'm too goddamn busy being fabulous to care. If, on the odd occasion, I do catch someone's gaze I more often than not smile in their direction. That, in itself, takes courage. Confidence. My smile is telling the world: 'Yes, go ahead, take a good look because I love who I am and I am proud to be me and that deserves attention!' Would you believe it, nine times out of ten I get a smile back. There is always one cranky arse, though, who doesn't, but I can guarantee those people are the sort to win the lottery and still have something to complain about, so you'd just be wasting your time with them anyhow.

I smile because I like smiling. When you grow up in the north-west of England it's practically written into your school curriculum. Lesson one, maths; lesson two, smiling and learning how to say 'heya love' to strangers; lesson three, science. I smile because I believe in being kind and, not to get too biblical, because two wrongs don't make a right. I also want people to go away with a positive experience of disability. I want to challenge their misconceptions. Of course, it's not my job but I want to do it.

Remember, be the person your younger self needed. I needed someone to tell the world that disability is beautiful, sexy, powerful, worthy of a smile not a stare. My hope is that perhaps next time instead of a stare they smile and pass on the smile train. Smiling certainly is contagious. I urge you all to try it today. Step out of your comfort zone and smile at a stranger. Okay, perhaps that's a little fantastical but I believe in the power of positivity. Ultimately, I want to teach others that I am a human just like you. Not an inanimate object for you to enjoy gawping at.

One of the biggest challenges is that non-disabled people feel so awkward around us. Their awkwardness radiates like a beacon and leaves many disabled people, me included, internalising the feeling of not belonging and being ashamed of our disabled bodies. The most powerful tool in combatting these feelings of internalised ableism, the unwanted attention and the objectification, has been to completely change my whole outlook and perception of the situation. A good old swaparoo, changing negative experiences into positive ones.

I was taught this lesson by Stephanie, the wise owl. It never ceases to amaze me how grounded and in tune with the world she is. We haven't always been best mates, but like any good sister she's always lifted me up in my darkest hours and there have been a good few, let me tell you. She is honest, pragmatic and sympathetic without being condescending.

So, Stephanie, my path to self-love and body confidence is very much down to your kind words in the car park at IKEA . . .

Let me set the scene. I am 17 or thereabouts, an emotional and hormone-fuelled time for anyone. For me, it is a time of utter confusion and transformation. I have broken away from the shackles of high school and, in many respects, have come into my own as I start college. New friends, a new look and no longer having to wear a school uniform all mean I can go wild with my clothes and make-up. Bright lipsticks, highlights and eyeliner galore.

My college is pretty decent. For the most part people are here to learn, a stark contrast to my high school, which just seemed like a never-ending popularity competition. Also, many of the pupils came from a low socio-economic background which sadly meant aspirations and the notion of dreaming big were not seen as a priority. But I do have big dreams and they are celebrated and seem possible at my new school.

The college is also much more diverse than my high school and I just don't stick out as much. I am able to blend in and just get on with things. I also experience a new-found independence. College means that I don't need a teaching assistant glued to my side in every class. Instead, I have more autonomy, being able to choose when and where I need any assistance. Pushing the parameters of what I think I can do. Taking risks. Becoming an independent young woman. Not this infantilised child that needs to be smothered and protected at all times.

I feel like a whole new me. I can finally breathe. I have also made some of the best friends a girl could ever have. Kate, Becca, Helen, Lydia, Katie B – you are all nothing short of the cheerleaders I had dreamed of. I have spent many a night, dreaming, manifesting you for years; you are all I wanted. A group of beautiful girls who see the beauty in me. As if by magic, here you are: intelligent, savvy and considerate. Nothing is too much for you all and I never feel like a burden in your company. If we want to go out for drinks, you find an accessible venue and form a shield of bodies around my wheelchair to push through the drunk crowds, edging our way through to the back of the bar to find a safe little corner so no one will fall on me. Blocking me from getting a cigarette burn on my face. My own personal bodyguards.

If I want to sleep at Becca's house after a girls' night out, you all find a way to hoist me up the stairs, even in our drunken state. And when we go on weekends away, even abroad, Kate, you methodically plan our trip and access needs from A to Z. Heck, the girls even think about which cars to purchase once they pass their driving tests so that my wheelchair will fit in their boot.

Of course, you all see my disability, and how disabling the world is, but you absolutely see Samantha first. I feel loved and safe in my college bubble, my besties at my side.

But I still can't control the outside world. I start to doubt whether I'll ever be accepted, and no amount of reinvention, blonde highlights or push-up bras can penetrate the layers of stereotypes, systemic ableism and oppression that come with being three feet tall and a wheelchair user. I kind of understand why I was treated like a child when I was a child, but now, almost an adult, people still ignore me.

The daily microaggressions and ignorant comments wear me down. The more independent I become, the more inequalities I encounter. The world is scary. I am starting to see it for what it truly is: a disabling and unaccommodating place. People still talk to me like I am unintelligent, as though my physical body impacts on my cognitive ability. 'Um, hello, I speak three languages – why are you using a patronising baby voice?'

I am still subjected to the side-tilt pity look and the label of the 'poor disabled person'. I am dumbfounded. There seems to be such a disconnect. I've proven you all wrong by getting this far and going to college, yet I am far from being seen as an equal. I am living in a world that, for the most part, doesn't really give a shit about disabled people or sees them as a burden. It terrifies me and it's more than my young mind can process.

On the one hand, I am flourishing within my newfound independence and freedom of expression, but at the same time I am battling depression. I have no drive. I feel helpless and cry at random moments. I feel decisions are being made for me in which I have no say. I still don't have a boyfriend. I had idealised what college would look like and that included dating. In many ways the rejection hurts more because, for once, I feel like the real me, not the fake version I conveyed in high school. If I am not seen as attractive being myself then this confirms my fears that I am unlovable. Something must be wrong with me.

My home life is also far from harmonious. Still battling with grief from my father's passing, Mama Renke is in a new relationship and there is talk of a move to France, potentially ripping me away from my new life. I feel helpless. I have visions of my mum and stepfather building a granny flat next to their villa and that's where I'll spend the rest of my years. Alone. Isolated. Without a voice or choice.

It feels like no one seems to care what I want. I become angry and bitter at the world, and I only see one thing to blame. My disabled body. I start to loathe being disabled. Everything I have ever wanted in life appears to be taken away from me as a direct cause of my disability. I see myself, my body, as the problem; not people's narrowmindedness, disablism or society's ignorance. Me.

This is a new feeling because I have always tried to embrace my uniqueness. Sure, I don't always feel like a ray of sunshine, but I have never hated myself. Now my innate sense of self and self-esteem just disappear. The inner voice that tells me I am pathetic, unlovable and hopeless speaks to me daily. It is amplified by the world around me. Nothing in society tells me my thoughts are unfounded. I mean, I haven't grown up seeing disabled people on television or in magazines. Even when I go to the shops, I never see anyone else in a wheelchair in Topshop or ASDA.

I go to the college counsellor. From the moment I enter her office, I sob uncontrollably, the sort of crying where you start to resemble Regan in *The Exorcist*, with snot streaming from your nose and not enough tissue paper to absorb it, so you have to use your sleeve. The counsellor is young, kind and softly spoken. She clearly tries her best to support me, but I quickly find that my frustration with ableism and my negative emotions about my disabled body appear new to her and our session turns more into me educating her about disability rather than something that empowers me. There is something she says, however, that sticks with me. I am so unbelievably insulted by her words that I never return.

'Why don't you talk to other disabled people, Samantha? Perhaps they can give you advice and comfort?'

The suggestion angers me; my mouth twists, I see red and I want to scream. Little do I know this is proof of how deep-rooted and insidious my internalised ableism is. I am not one of 'them'. In fact, I want nothing to do with anyone disabled.

Part of the college was given over to people with severe cognitive disabilities. Other students used to take the piss out of them. I felt the counsellor was lumping me in with them. I didn't see myself in them and it made me angry that she somehow did.

Now, this book isn't about regrets, yet I often wonder what would have been if I had taken her advice then and there. Because my life now is so empowered and enriched by my disability community. Perhaps I wouldn't have felt so alone. Perhaps I would have been listened to like never before. Perhaps. But I'm not one for guessing games. This was my path and I wasn't ready for this life lesson, not just yet anyway.

For anyone who has battled depression, you will know that life becomes grey and you find yourself going through the motions. Surviving not thriving. Numb. I put on a brave face in front of my girlfriends, something I have mastered since childhood. No one wants a miserable disabled kid, even when they lie in a hospital bed. But anything outside of my social interactions means nothing to me. Even a trip to IKEA – which is normally met with excitement, a highlight for any youngster and, let's face it, any self-respecting adult – doesn't spark joy. No amount of Swedish meatballs and crap you don't really need but buy in abundance anyway penetrates this incredibly sad and frightened Samantha.

'Come on get ready, we're going to IKEA,' says Mama Renke.

The last thing I want is to be around other people but I am not to be left alone at home. I am dragged along. All I remember of that day are people's eyes on me. No more than usual but I feel them like lasers cutting through my flesh. Now, I can't recall my exact words, but afterwards I seek validation and reassurance from my family. I want to know that it isn't all in my head, that people are really being rude.

'Did you see them staring?' I ask, bursting into tears in the car park. My sister kneels by my side.

'Have you perhaps thought about why they are staring?'

What a stupid question and not at all helpful!

'Because they are dickheads,' I say.

'Perhaps,' Stephanie says. 'But maybe, just maybe, you've got it all wrong. Perhaps they are staring because you have the best sense of style and not because you are in a wheelchair? You have such a sense of style, Samantha, you always look so well put together: effortless and sleek. I could never imagine dressing like you do. It's a skill not many people have. I wish I did and I'm rather envious. Perhaps that's why they're staring?'

I am taken aback, first because my sister is giving me a compliment, which doesn't happen that often. I am always somewhat jealous of her achievements and beauty. I never think I can measure up, let alone be someone she admires. I am also taken aback because I have honestly never thought of it like that. I've always assumed the worst. I'm in bright red lipstick and a hat. She is right; I am bloody good at fashion. So why wouldn't people stare at this young fashionista in all her glory in the most mundane of places, IKEA?

If people are going to stare, give them something to stare at . . .

The truth is I will never know what goes on in other people's minds. Perhaps they are staring because of my disability. Perhaps they are staring because they don't expect a disabled person to care about their appearance and put on red lipstick. Perhaps they are staring because they want to know what shade of lipstick I am wearing and where I got my outfit from because I look beautiful, and they want to replicate it.

Either way, I am the one in control and I am the one who decides how another person's actions make me feel. Now, wherever I am and wherever I go, I remember my sister's words. Even when I'm having the toughest of days and I catch someone staring at me, I remember not to always go to a dark place. I remind myself that I am beautiful, and I deserve to be the centre of attention.

No one has the right to dictate your worth. To objectify your body. To make you feel like you aren't beautiful. Choose to believe in yourself. Change the narrative. Take control of the situation and tell the world you have nothing to feel ashamed of because your uniqueness deserves to be on show. Our bodies may change but our worth remains the same.

That said, it's okay to grieve about your changing body if you need to. Because allowing myself to pull out a teeny violin from time to time has brought me peace when my body lets me down the most. Grieving is part of the disability experience, yet we don't get to talk about it because we are often told how brave we are, how great it is that we've overcome our disability, how resilient we are and how strong we are being all the time.

This leaves us very little room to express how we are really feeling, which can at times make us feel incredibly lonely. Chin up, don't cry, it will be okay – otherwise known as toxic positivity. Well, sometimes I'm not okay and I want to take time out to grieve. Every time I fracture a bone, I grieve. I grieve the loss of my body as it was prior to the fracture. With every fracture comes the emotional trauma. The temporary impact on my independence. Bed rest; not being able to propel my wheelchair. Going round and round as I try to push my chair with one arm, the other tied up in a sling. I grieve the absence of pain. I grieve the happy Samantha who, for about a week or so, disappears and is replaced by a rather nasty and grumpy She-Hulk, mostly due to the side-effects of opioids. I mean, I can't be Mother Teresa all the time now, can I?

I also grieve the loss of function. This is the short-term period until my bone has healed, perhaps six to eight weeks, depending on the severity. Then there's the long-term loss of function. You see, my bone is pretty shoddy and, even though I do heal, the new bone callus is often super-weak and clumpy. Think of a tree branch: snap it in two, then use papier maché to try to bridge it back together. What you are left with is a very unstable, clunky and deformed-looking bone. You probably wouldn't notice unless I tried to stretch both my arms out, but they both look more like boomerangs than straight lines.

Fun fact: I was originally right-handed, my right arm being the dominant side. But this dominance came at a price: as a young infant with brittle bones my arm would fracture over and over. It deformed and twisted so often and so much that I learned to write with my left hand instead. Every time I break a bone, I also run the risk of losing just a little bit more mobility; that inch I so desperately need to push my wheelchair or to reach that shelf may be taken away and I will have to learn to move and navigate a different way, perhaps introducing more mobility aids into my life. Finding a new way of transferring from my wheelchair to the toilet, for example, or relying on others more to help with tasks.

You don't, however, need to have a disability to experience this grief. Our bodies never stop changing; our cells regenerate every seven to ten years and, essentially, we become new people. Women can see their bodies change during the menstrual cycle or when they have a baby. We may acquire scars, food intolerances, stretch marks, hair loss, and gain or lose weight. Change can absolutely be a blessing – a new job, home or partner – but when change happens to our bodies, the aesthetics are there for the whole world to pass judgement on and it can sometimes be a hard pill to swallow. How can we make sure this new version is celebrated and respected, and not something we come to dislike about ourselves?

I've found over the years that the body can be the most powerful thing we have in our life. Its ability to heal, for example. I mean, pick a scab and see the wonders of the body first-hand. We are fascinating, complex machines. We've all had those nights when we've drunk our body weight in booze and quite literally polluted ourselves. Yet our body forgives us for this abuse by eventually flushing the toxins away and the following day we are back on the lash.

I've certainly seen my body bounce back from being cut open from one end to another and having metal wire drilled into it. So, it can come as a real blow when our sacred vessels don't bounce back or work as we'd hoped. Our body changing can blindside us and, in many ways, we can feel totally abandoned by the one thing supposed to protect us above all. As I recently found out . . .

I am sitting here toothless. Nope, that's not some cool, down-with-the-kids analogy (I wish it were). My teeth are falling out of my mouth and it's something I'm struggling with. My body – once again taking me by surprise – is changing without warning. Now, as I run my tongue along my teeth, all I feel are gaps, chips and cracks, which comes with an overwhelming feeling of sadness and despair.

Losing one's teeth – that's what nightmares are made of, right? I'm sure we've all had those horrendous, sweat-drenched dreams in which we lose all our teeth and then we wake up, flustered and panicked, and immediately stick our entire fist in our mouth to make sure every last molar is still intact. I know there have been times when I've Googled 'what does it mean when we dream about our teeth falling out?', only to find out it means we are stressed and overworked. Well, this nightmare has become a reality for me, and it sucks balls.

Having brittle bones, which is a collagen deficiency, affects every inch of my body, from my toenails to my heart, my hair follicles to my bronchi. Around 50 per cent of those with osteogenesis imperfecta also have something called dentinogenesis imperfecta, which basically means the teeth are über-brittle, like my bones. Ironically, even though my teeth have always been small and discoloured due to the lack of dentine, I have never had any problems. In fact, I love going to the dentist because I always get a sticker. I've never once had a filling, never mind any teeth falling out, and no real trauma.

That was up until about four years ago, when I woke up in agony from one of my front bottom teeth. I think I knew immediately what had happened. I also knew I was heading off to Mexico on holiday two days later and really didn't want to have to book an emergency appointment. It was totally one of those ostrich-head-in-the-sand moments. I convinced myself that, if I ignored it, it would go away.

But it got worse. I could actually wiggle the tooth with my tongue. I was looking at it in the mirror every five minutes. 'It's not broken, just sore gums ... an infection, maybe?' Who the fuck am I kidding? The tooth is swaying from side to side with ease. The morning of my trip I am in unbearable pain. A private dentist confirms my worst nightmare.

'It needs to come out, Samantha,' the dentist says.

'Like now? Now?' is all I can manage.

Devastated, mortified, enraged. All the feelings you can imagine that come with being in your early thirties and losing a front tooth.

To say that losing my front tooth put a downer on my Mexican hoopla is an understatement. There is no sarong or sexy bikini or pina colada that can convince me I am attractive. I spend most of my holiday perfecting my ventriloquism act, barely moving my mouth. Paper napkins are my new best friend, acting as a shield in front of my mouth. I'm sure the locals just think I am being a quintessentially British lady, demurely hiding her face, but the truth is all I can think about is that they might be making comments about teeth. After all, I'd made such comments myself in the past. 'Gosh, look at those hillbillies' or 'only druggies lose all their teeth, right?'

I keep thinking about my career, which is just starting to take off. How on earth can I go on camera with no teeth? I keep repeating a story someone told me about a recent date with a fellow who had missing and chipped teeth after a motorbike accident and how she couldn't get past his appearance, so decided not to see him any more. Why me, why now? It isn't fair and I deserve better than to be in my thirties and having to explain why I've got Poligrip beside the lipstick in my Louis Vuitton clutch.

Then it hits me: shit, what about kissing? Heck, what about giving a blow job? What if a denture falls out in the act or gets stuck to his foreskin? You aren't supposed to sleep with dentures in so what am I supposed to do? Sneak them out once my partner's fallen asleep and wake up early and pop them in? Keep them under my pillow?

The nightmare went on for a few years, losing more teeth and unable to have corrective implants because of my weak jaw. Each tooth loss skyrocketed me into a deep sadness and anxiety. I withdrew. I wouldn't eat out in public in case my denture popped out.

The anger and disappointment I felt towards my body left me feeling bitter. Why had it decided to do this, particularly when everything else in my life seemed to be on the up? All I could see was darkness.

Then I had a moment of clarity; I took the opportunity to appear as a guest panellist on a morning TV show to highlight my tooth loss. I knew I couldn't be alone and, heck, if a viewer or a good orthodontist had any advice to offer, then what was there to lose? Instead, I received abuse online and comments from vicious trolls, mocking me about my teeth. Like a little snail, I crumbled and retreated into my shell. I never wanted to talk about it again. I just wanted to suffer in silence. It was a very lonely few years.

I've learned over the years that the things I hate the most about my body – like my asymmetrical boobs or my translucent, discoloured and brittle teeth – come from people telling me I should feel embarrassed or ashamed. That I'm not good enough.

I think back to when I started to feel self-conscious about my teeth. I think I was about 13 and a boy in the school cafeteria came up to me out of nowhere and said: 'Do you even have teeth?' Absolutely mortified, I went home and sat for hours looking at my smile in the mirror. Up until then I hadn't paid any attention or given much thought to my teeth or how they were objects of curiosity.

If that boy hadn't pointed out my teeth that time, perhaps my current situation wouldn't be weighing so heavily on my shoulders? I think about how I see my scars on my body and I have a completely different outlook about those. I have multiple scars running the length of my spine and my legs. Deep, thick scars – and I love them. They are my badges of honour. Each scar tells the story of a moment in history, a part of my life, and I don't associate them with pain or suffering but strength and courage. They are a part of my unique self.

So where am I now with my teeth? I spent years feeling desperately hopeless about my tooth loss. Then, one day, I just stopped. I guess because I was done letting other people's judgements rule over my life. I remember the day: nothing extraordinary, I was finishing brushing my teeth and about to position my mini-denture when I stopped, looked dead at the mirror and opened my mouth, all the gaps on display. I hadn't done this for a long time without my denture already in place.

I looked in the mirror and talked directly to myself. I was so tired of feeling angry at my body. I needed to make peace with the situation.

'Well, you are fucking gone now, aren't you? Literally nothing I can do to change what has been.'

Once I did this, I was able to be more pragmatic about my next steps. I asked a friend to suggest a dentist who could help, and I reached out to other people with my condition to see if they could offer any advice. I changed my mindset and, once again, things became clearer. I wasn't in pain as I once had been and, dare I say, I became excited about owning a new set of gnashers. I had been unhappy with my discoloured teeth for a long time and – if I really didn't have much control as to whether or not they were going to continue to fall out – then I would just replace them with a pearly white smile. Heck, the prospect of some nice new teeth, even if they did need to be fixed with Poligrip, wasn't so bad after all. In fact, it actually made me smile for the first time in a long time.

Listen, I didn't pop out of my mother's lady garden with 'The Sound of Music' playing as the theme tune to my life. I don't wake up each morning like a Disney princess, with birds and squirrels singing in perfect harmony with me. Usually, I wake up to the stench of cat poo and I stretch and let out the loudest fart you can imagine.

Like everyone else, sometimes I get frustrated with my body. I dip in and out of fad diets. I compare myself to literally everyone on Instagram and I get annoyed that I now have to carry Poligrip with me everywhere. Nevertheless, and with my hand on my heart, most days I like, even love, my body. Yes, I love and am grateful for my disabled body. I love how it keeps up with my busy mind, my thirst for adventure and my never-ending aspirations. Its resilience. The fact that it is not even four feet high in total, it has experienced trauma over and over again, but despite all that it keeps plodding on.

I love how it talks to me and, even when it's broken, it shows me new ways of challenging myself. I haven't always had this positive attitude, mind you. In fact, it's only really since I hit 30 that I have been able to be completely butt naked and admire my curves, my wonky boobs and my shortened limbs in the mirror and say, 'Yup, that'll do.'

Respecting and appreciating your body doesn't have to mean it's your best friend every day. Loving your body can simply be about appreciating the fact that it allows you to be present, in the moment, breathing, alive.

When was the last time you thanked your body? I have to confess I tend to do so only after a fall, ill health or an operation. I'm grateful that my tiny little shell has once again allowed me to see another day and I am often amazed by its ability to bounce back. 'Thank you for giving me another day on this earth,' I whisper.

I am, however, trying to practise gratitude and thank my body more often. I mean, take a moment and think about how simply magical it is. We are as complex as a galaxy – doesn't that just blow your mind? We come into this world with just our body; it is our soulmate, our number-one companion throughout our life. So why not be kind to it, praise and worship it?

If you think about all the things you aren't too keen on about your body, you'll probably find that it is because someone has made you feel inadequate about them in the past. Or that you have absorbed the idea that your body doesn't fit societal norms of beauty. Or because your health or disability has taken a downward turn and your life is in a state of flux. Just remember that *you* aren't the problem. Your body isn't the issue. You are beautiful.

So, to all the toothless, wonky-boobed, bendy-penised, hairless, curvy, freckled beauties out there, we are uniquely ourselves and we should be proud of that fact. Because our worth is not dependent on the approval of others.

8

Am I Enough?

'Good things come in small packages.'

You deserve love, respect and dignity. That's not a cliché, just a straight-up, solid fact. We all need human connection, some more than others. The bottom line is we all want to feel loved. Heard. Worthy. Worthy enough for another human being to notice us and see all the beauty we have to offer this world. A partner in crime, someone to create memories, share passions and smile with. Just to clarify, I'm totally not ruling out pets when I say this.

Yet sometimes we lose ourselves in the pursuit of love when, in fact, we need to learn to love ourselves before anyone else. I believe it was Mama Ru Paul who said: 'If you can't love yourself, how in the hell you gonna love somebody else?' I'm sure as hell not going to argue with Mama Ru!

Remember I told you I'm like cookie dough, not yet fully baked? One of those Millie's cookies, soft and gooey in the middle and crunchy on the outside? Well, there are some areas of my life where I'm totally smashing it, where I've got the bull by its horns. Then there are others where I feel so lost and vulnerable that I often want to curl up in the foetal position and drink wine until I pass out. Of course, if I do I'll end up being woken up by Bruno the cat sitting on my head with his testicles strategically perched on my lips. Yup, that's right, I have on more than one occasion been teabagged by my Sphynx.

I'm totally a work in progress and still have moments of utter despair and loneliness. No more so than when it comes to relationships and dating. I guess I don't want to be seen as a stereotype. I've had enough of those for one lifetime. I don't want another side head-tilt from someone who assumes I'm alone and undatable because I'm in a wheelchair. The disabled chick who can't get laid. That's so far from the truth – I'm totally datable and fuckable. I mean, getting laid isn't the issue here. Rather, it's the feelings of not being deserving of love that stop me dead in my wheels.

I grew up, like many young girls, watching Disney, waiting around for my prince to sweep me off my feet so I can live happily ever after. I've always seen myself as a good catch: bright, funny, witty and confident, comfortable expressing my sexuality. Yet as the years went by, and all my friends started to get boyfriends, get married and start families, I began battling with the feeling that I would never be deserving of love and that I would never get my happy ending.

But, Samantha, you've had sex; you've had relationships. Surely you are confident! This is true, but I am also the product of a society that doesn't believe in my worth when it comes to love, sex or the ability to have meaningful relationships. Like many things in my life, I have internalised that shit.

Over the years I've ingested the ideas set by society that dictate how I should be as a disabled person. I have absolutely lowered my expectation when it comes to dating, sex and even motherhood. I still have moments when I truly believe that all the above are exclusive to non-disabled folk and simply too far out of my reach. That I should just be happy for others and accept that I cannot have any of these wonders.

At my lowest point, I will see a cute guy and tell myself not to bother smiling at him because he wouldn't date someone in a wheelchair. I roll right past when really I should smile, wink and say to myself he'd be lucky to be in my life. Instead, the fun, flirty and confident Samantha I love disappears and I become unrecognisable. Beaten down by painful self-loathing.

In these moments I'm a numb, hollow shell. But who can blame me? The charity Scope reports that only 5 per cent of people who aren't disabled have ever asked out, or been on a date with, a disabled person. You can see why I don't always 'feel the love'.

I cannot remember a time when friends or family have asked if I'm dating or even if I'd like to become a mother one day. These conversations seem to be reserved for non-disabled people. Awkwardness around disability prevails. Of course, I don't think people intentionally try to exclude me, but it is another little nail in the coffin that internalises my ableist thoughts that I am not deserving of love. Or, sometimes, disabled people are on the receiving end of the opposite response: people cannot believe your relationship is real; your partner must be a caregiver, sibling or a friend, but never the lover you just had anal sex with hours before. So much to navigate on top of finding your way in the maze of dating etiquette.

I give myself such a hard time about it as well. In many ways I am a little disappointed in myself; I feel so empowered in some areas of my life yet, in the same breath, I allow others to make me feel completely unlovable, scared and not good enough. It's like I'm two totally different people where dating is concerned. Honestly, if I didn't have brittle bones, I'd shake myself. I've often slipped into a dark hole of self-deprecation, undoing all the wonderful self-love and time I've invested in myself.

Rejection – or simply the notion of it – terrifies me and it is absolutely my sticking point. I even question those individuals who ask me out or flirt with me. Why date me? Is this a joke? Are they screen-grabbing our conversations and laughing about the little disabled chick online?

I don't want this chapter to seem like a total contradiction or a cop-out, but living with a disability is, in many ways, a life that is constantly battling contradictions. Disability culture and identity is a mind-fuck. You can feel so proud of your uniqueness one minute and the next those years of microaggressions, oppression and internalised ableism creep up seemingly out of nowhere and you start to doubt everything, including yourself.

You spend many a day simply wading through all these conflicting notions to try to find out how and where you fit. You can totally think you are the best thing since sliced bread and have bags of self-worth then pop out for a drink with a friend on a Friday night and be told you can't enter a bar because it's full and you, as a wheelchair user, are a 'fire risk'. Or you can encounter that drunken group of people who start to heckle you, pointing and taking pictures because you are disabled, ruining your night. And even when your friends try to comfort you by saying you should ignore them, all you hear is toxic positivity, dismissing your feelings. Because what you really want is for the world to recognise the barriers you face instead of feeling awkward around disability. It can be so hard sometimes to see your worth in a society that clearly doesn't recognise it.

I want this chapter to reflect the reality of what it's like to be physically disabled and a woman living in a world where we still place value on a woman's ability to please a man/partner, to be a mother and a good wife. I will have guys dismiss me as a partner because they assume I cannot have sex or bear children, as though my worth is inherently entwined with these qualities.

Sure, we've come a long way and relationships and gender norms aren't binary any longer, but the pressure of living up to all of the above is intense. Trust me, I think about it a lot and I'm working super-hard to try to figure out what truly makes me happy and what I want when it comes to being in a relationship.

So, without further ado, here's my unapologetic truth about dating and sex.

I've been a one-night stand, a friend, but never a girl-friend. A fetish, a dirty little secret, a sexting partner, a phone sex collaborator, a drunk gay man's curiosity fumble, a workplace flirtation, a curiosity fuck. Oh, and the recipient of many a 'I think you're great, but . . .' I've been a target of predators, I've had my wheelchair turned into a weapon so someone could grope me, and I've been a distraction from someone's stale relationship.

I've been all of these things, but I've never simply been someone's number one. Sometimes, just some-times, that makes me rather sad.

My battle with my lack of confidence when it comes to relationships is a complex one and some of those complexities are directly linked to my disability. I'd be a liar if I didn't acknowledge the glaring barriers and ableist attitudes I encounter as a disabled woman when dating. First, many non-disabled people don't even see disabled people as being sexual and sensual individuals. If only I had a penny for every time someone has asked me if I can even have sex. I guess it's because disabled people are often viewed in this almost childlike state: innocent, helpless, like a puppy or small child. We are often infantilised, a belief that is perpetuated by the media. I mean, can you remember the last time you watched a sex scene with disabled people on main-stream television?

All of this spills out into everyday interactions. As a society, we are influenced by this insidious smog, day in, day out. It is why I advocate and scream from the roof-tops that we need more authentic representation of disabled people. I want to see disabled boobs and bums just as much as I want to see disabled people as moth-ers, lovers, rebels and professionals, because our lives are shaped by these harmful stereotypes and it bloody sucks. It means we constantly have to rectify people's preconceptions and justify who we are. It is so draining and frustrating.

Then there's the whole curiosity surrounding our anatomy. Do we or don't we have bits and, if so, do they work? I swear some people see a wheelchair and assume we all look like Barbies and Kens under our clothes, a little bump where our genitals should be. I've joked in the past that I should wear a T-shirt that reads 'FYI, I CAN HAVE SEX' because I'd always be overlooked by guys in bars or at social engagements who simply wouldn't deem me to be good dating stock or who'd come up to me and ask for a high five as though they were talking to a younger sibling. The T-shirt thing is ludicrous but it still upsets me that I feel the need to even have to offer that kind of personal information to a stranger just so they might feel more comfortable and see me as 'normal'.

Still now I find myself slipping into a mindset of pleasing others, of being transparent and open right from the get-go with the opposite sex about my sexual capabilities, or of flirting outrageously, using my humour to fling sexual innuendoes left, right and centre in the hope of dispelling the myth that disabled people can't have sex or date. Sure, people think I'm hilarious and sassy and the fellas love my crude nature, but it's not me. It is my alter ego. The Samantha still battling her internalised ableism.

No woman should have to feel like they need to be sexual to deserve respect or attention. For so many years I yearned for a sexual connection so I could feel 'normal'. This desire to please others and to be socially accepted has, however, left me in some pretty vulnerable and scary situations. I've never had sex without being pretty drunk first because, in all honesty, I've never really wanted to go through with any of the sexual experiences but have never been brave or comfortable enough simply to say, 'No, I'm okay waiting until I feel truly relaxed and happy.'

Thankfully, I no longer feel the need to have intimate relationships to feel worthy and normal, but this has only been a recent development. I've not had sex for four years. This includes two years of a global pandemic and lockdowns, of course, which saw me living back home with Mama Renke (no hanky panky going on under her roof). But although I've had opportunities in that time, I've recognised that the after-effects of feeling numb and inadequate aren't worth it.

Part of me feels like I am not experienced enough, and this will show. I've also been reminded on many occasions that I am 'wrong' during sex. I bled during a one-night stand and the guy couldn't get out of the door fast enough. He was convinced I was a virgin because I was disabled; he assumed I had lured him over to have my one night of passion and pop my cherry. He was actually number three on my tally of sexual partners but my tilted cervix means I bleed sometimes.

Then there was the guy who became rather frustrated – almost angry – that my vagina was 'too tight', and he refused to use lube to resolve this 'issue'. I will let that sink in with you for a moment because I wasn't aware that having a small vagina was a negative. I mean, aren't there rap songs literally praising tight pussies? Also, come on now, mate, I'm three feet something tall, so of course my lady bits are going to be a little more compact. But that doesn't mean we can't talk and work together to accommodate both our wants and desires.

Initially, I came away from these experiences really pissed off and also feeling a little embarrassed, my internalised ableism whispering in my ear again, but actually now I'm grateful. It did me a favour – because I now know about myself and how comfortable I feel about my body and my disability identity and I have come to see these interactions for what they were. They were just another way society was trying to push the narrative that I was wrong, that I wasn't normal and I was the problem. I am not wrong; I am unique and I am definitely not a problem. And my vagina is fucking amazing, thank you very much!

Being someone's curiosity fuck or being overlooked by the opposite sex is never easy, but – without condoning it – I weirdly kind of get it. Why? Because, once upon a time, I too was ignorant.

The truth is, sex scares me. Terrifies me, in fact. Apologies in advance to all my sexual partners, who may or may not be reading this, but I've never truly enjoyed having sex. I guess at 36 that may come as a surprise to some. I'm sure many would simply say that I've not found 'the one', but it goes deeper than finding a strong connection with a person. My fear of sex and intimacy goes back to childhood. For a very long time I didn't even think I could have sex.

'Can you kiss a boy, Sam, or will you break your jaw? Can you imagine if you had sex? The penis would come out through your mouth!'

The unsavoury comments would flow during high school, but I didn't have an answer to those questions. Instead, I only had the overwhelming urge to want to be seen as 'normal' and to defend myself.

'Of course, I can have sex,' I'd snap back with absolute certainty, disgusted that they'd even think otherwise, but these comments stayed with me for days, whirling around in my mind. The sheer panic. What if I can't? What if my body is too small or I break a bone? Will I grow boobs? What if I don't get my period? Can I have children? These are all things an 11-year-old shouldn't really be concerned by or obsessing over.

If the boys in school thought I couldn't even kiss, then I'd never have a boyfriend. From a young age, I was resigned to the fact that I'd be alone and undatable. Ironically, around this time I'd learn the word *spinster* in a history class. I was convinced it was how I would end up.

I guess many of us have fallen into the trap during high school of putting all our time and energy into fitting in. Being a sheep not a unicorn. Following the others. Trying not to stand out. I look back without regret, however, because I was doing the only thing I knew to survive high school. I spent an enormous amount of time trying to be like everyone else and, ultimately, attempting to get the boys' attention. Not necessarily because I wanted a boyfriend or fancied any of them (okay, maybe one), but because I thought that I only had any worth or value if someone else saw it. If

someone proclaimed to the world that I was their someone. Being in a relationship was synonymous with being
normal, or so I thought.

The more rejection I received, the more I believed
what the doctors had said at my birth. There was something wrong with me and the whole world knew it.

I wasn't a popular kid, nor was I unpopular or a
geek, as we would often refer to kids who didn't fit the
high-school norms. Ironically, these are the kids who
often end up being the most interesting. I suppose I
was an all-rounder. I was cheeky and funny and not
shy. I gave as good as I got and, in some ways, I guess
that gave me street cred. My mid-grade popularity
afforded me some invites to school parties. Like any
teenager, I'd have to buy a new outfit and plan weeks
ahead, feeling pretty darn chuffed that I'd been
accepted into their world. I'd make myself look as
attractive as I could to get noticed, rocking a red-frilled
Tammy Girl dress and a tiara. (Yes, I totally wore a
tiara – it made me feel like a princess.) But often I left
these parties heartbroken.

Although some of the lads in my class would chat
and even dance with me, they'd all splinter off when the
slow songs came on, snogging other girls in the class or
attempting the odd fingering in the corner. Gosh, all I
ever wanted at age 13 was to get fingered at a party. Not
so much for the physical pleasure, but so I would have
something relatable to contribute during lunch break

with my girlfriends. Really, was that too much to ask? But it never happened. I was sick of being on the periphery. I wanted in on the action. I wanted my friends to swoon around me with excitement that I had got a snog. I wanted to be like them.

I knew some of the lads in my class liked me. From time to time they would even hold hands with me under the table – but never in front of anyone. Never publicly. Because, even then, the boys knew they would get the piss taken out of them for dating the 'crip' in the chair. Look, I get it, high school is brutal and what your friends think of you feels like the most important thing in the world, but that doesn't mean I've forgotten how it felt to be 13-year-old Samantha and have others feel embarrassed about me.

I've realised that rejection – or even the trauma of a possible rejection – is my kryptonite. I simply don't allow myself to be in a position where it can happen. This means I simply don't date much. I don't allow myself to be hurt, but in doing so I can't move forward. I realise I'm tarnishing the whole male species with the same brush so why not get my head out of my fanny and get over it? I guess because I'm human and being hurt, over and over, takes time to heal. It hurts to be that girl who was never asked out or that young woman who got laughed at and pointed at by lads in a bar.

Being proactive is something I pride myself on. Control gives me a sense of calm. But I cannot control if someone finds me attractive or not. I cannot control if someone has been indoctrinated by years of misinformation about disability. So, for a long time, I simply didn't allow anyone the chance to give an opinion. Every now and then, over the years, I have let my guard down and permitted a wave of assertiveness to wash over me, even on the odd occasion putting myself out there by channelling my inner Carrie from *Sex and the City*. I'm fabulous and anyone who doesn't see that be damned. But this enthusiasm often wavered fast as the rejections persisted.

Simply being on dating apps can throw off my sense of worth before even meeting a guy. The complexity of online dating means you can often find yourself feeling as though you need to mask your disability identity because of the 'swipe away' culture of objectification that it promotes. I find myself internally debating and torturing myself as to whether I should disclose my disability online.

Now I'm sure some of you are yelling out 'YES, of course you should!' and I totally get why you'd think that because I am proud of my disability identity. But my inner voice stops me, based on years of people seeing my wheelchair before they see the person using it. In the outside world, people can make snap judgements based on my appearance, but online I have the power to control my own narrative. In some ways that's liberating, even when it's steeped in another form of oppression.

Having to mask my disability online may seem like a complete lack of empowerment, but I believe feeling empowered comes in all shapes and sizes. You can only feel like you own a situation when you are completely comfortable and, if that means taking baby steps, then I'm all for it. We all navigate situations differently and we should never shame anyone into taking leaps they simply aren't ready for. All we can do is be there to listen and respect one another. Plus, it also makes for one heck of a social experiment.

My approach thus far has been to upload a photo that doesn't show my wheelchair, see who fancies a chat and then whittle these individuals down to my top five. Once I've been chatting for a few days I disclose my disability. Initially, I do feel empowered and in control but, overall, I wish I didn't have to operate this way as it doesn't make for pleasant dating, let me tell you.

For a short time, presenting yourself like this means you release yourself from societal prejudices, but ultimately you lose who you are and that's not good for the soul. You find yourself on edge all the time because you have this strange feeling of being a fraud or deceiving the other person. A criminal. However, who knows what the other person is also choosing not to tell you about just so that they can be themselves without any labels? Perhaps an ex-wife, children or an obsession with trains?

So why do I always feel so guilty for not sharing my disability? Why do I feel like a catfish? I guess, above all, I feel like when I do this I let myself down. I should lead by example and practise what I preach: that being disabled isn't a bad thing but is part of what makes me beautiful. I shouldn't let others dictate my worth but instead I should challenge their ignorance and try to educate others.

But can you blame me? It's never easy to receive comments like 'Gosh, you are brave to be on here'. Or 'So can you move your legs then?' Or 'Are you a midget?' Or 'I've never fucked someone like you!' Or simply being blocked after you share your truth.

I guess I should look at this objectively and see the other side of the coin. What is the worst that could happen if I am loud and proud? Yes, I may receive ignorant and offensive comments or encounter people making snap judgements and swiping me away. But I might just connect with someone who is incredible, who sees me for me and we live happily ever after.

Then there are the practicalities of being disabled and dating. Having a disability means you spend an awful lot of money on things that other people, I suppose, take for granted, like travel. I once met a guy online and, after chatting for a while, I duly disclosed my disability. He said he was cool with it, so we decided to meet for a drink. As I struggle getting on public transport independently, I often travel by taxi. In London, black taxis are all fully accessible, but they are a luxury in the sense that you pay a premium. So, where others may have hopped on a bus or the Underground to meet this guy, I paid over £40 for a round trip in a black cab.

We drank and we ate, but then the words you never really want to hear came out.

'I think we should just be friends,' he said.

It had taken so much courage, energy and money to meet with this guy that I snapped.

'I don't really need any more friends, thanks.'

He ordered one more drink and then left. Oh yes, and he left me holding the entire bill. I was so distraught I sat crying at the table. Luckily, it was a restaurant I'd been to frequently, and they took pity on me and halved the bill. On the way out, in my despair, I interrupted a couple's date to share my drunken story, tears rolling down my face. Then I tried to lure the bouncer back to my flat on the way out, slipping my phone number into his hand. Not my finest moment, granted, but the thought of the money and time I'd wasted that night just added more evidence to my already negative view of dating. I concluded I'd rather spend the money on clothes and things that bring me joy.

The cost of dating, the inaccessibility of most venues, the ignorant remarks and the simple act of being ignored by the opposite sex are all shitty and don't leave you feeling that great about the dating game. But this pales in comparison to being fetishised and targeted by some just because they want to fuck a small person or one with a disability.

This can vary from someone simply being curious to the kind of guys who see women as conquests, who go from woman to woman picking them out because they have a unique quality, like they're on a tick-off list. Or the predatory individuals who clearly like the fact that your appearance is 'young'. Or those who get off on disability, who are often described as 'devotees'.

I've experienced them all and on each occasion it has made me feel so vulnerable. To be clear, this isn't about demonising anyone for their sexual preference. This isn't saying that consenting adults cannot do whatever the heck they want. We can all have a preference and enjoy kinky fantasies we'd perhaps rather not share with others outside the realms of our sex lives. Heck, it has been brought to my attention that I am a niche market and, if I ever fancied a career in porn or as a dominatrix, it would be rather lucrative.

I've never obliged, but during my early years in London, when money was tight and the acting career was slow, I did seriously consider it. I mean, nothing hardcore – just perhaps bulk-buying 99-pence knickers from Primark, wearing them for a day or two, then selling them to the highest bidder. I've even come close to accepting a 'paypig' request – I do love to dress up in sexy leather and beautiful lingerie, with red lips and big hair.

The problem comes when you aren't in control and, unknowingly and unwillingly, you become someone's fetish. It becomes non-consensual. You are objectified and that can leave you feeling once again like you're not good enough. It makes you feel like a freak, not a person, and I do not use the word lightly. To illustrate the minefield that is dating I will tell you a story . . .

It had been a month since we'd slept together, and I certainly wasn't going to be the one to message him. After all, he technically had just started seeing someone else. Nothing serious, he assured me, and in fact I was also casually dating at the time. That hadn't happened in years, so you can imagine I felt like the cat who got the cream when I found myself to be the interest of not one guy but two.

What we had was completely spontaneous. A night of passion that had caught us both off-guard. And it was sexy as hell. Starting in a restaurant, in the taxi ride home, and then back at mine. I hadn't felt so alive in a long time. Maybe I'm not undatable? The confidence boost was what I thought I'd needed.

As quickly as it began, however, it was over. We decided not to see each other again, both wanting to see what happened with the partners we were dating, although I craved the feeling of being alive so much that I desperately wanted a rematch. A few weeks went by and nothing, then, out of the blue, his name appears on my screen. I feel that tingling sensation down below. I hesitate to message back. I have a film crew waiting for me downstairs as I am doing a cameo appearance in a

Paloma Faith music video. (I know, my life is random as shit at times and I really can't do with a distraction right now.)

Clearly without willpower, I message back. The text quickly escalates from a casual 'hey, how have you been?' to 'tell me what you want to do to me'.

He says he wants to dress me up, dress me up young.

Immediately a deep pit forms in my stomach. I know where this is heading because, deep down, I knew this was all too good to be true. I try to divert the conversation.

'You mean like Britney Spears? I could totally rock the schoolgirl outfit, sexy lingerie.'

'No,' he replies, 'younger than that. How do you feel about wearing a nappy?'

Internalised ableism, infantilisation, being spoken to in a patronising and condescending manner – from my teachers to my doctor to the lady on the till at the post office. I've worked so hard to be seen as the intellectual, determined, sexual and sensational human being I am for years and years. To be treated with dignity, respect and to be loved for the whole me, not just my disability. To be asked to dress up as a baby when I am only three feet something tall was a kick in the teeth and made me feel dirty. I wanted just once to be seen as a badass, sexy grown woman.

Why couldn't he find me sexy without fetishising me? My response was one I'm proud of. I could have succumbed to his request, as I have so many times before. Engaging in his desire to feel like a grown up. So I could prove people wrong and dispel the myth that disabled people don't have sex.

My cheeks burning, my stomach doing somersaults and with a deep, deep, sense of sadness, I replied.

'If you see it from my point of view, it's a little demoralising, particularly if all your life you've fought to be treated like an adult. I'd rather turn someone on for seeing me as a sexy woman. I've had a lot of devotees in the past approach me, and it's just something I've never felt comfortable with. I'd like to be more than a fetish.'

I wiped away my tears, touched up my make-up, went downstairs and performed for the cameras. Smiles galore. The song was so aptly entitled 'Warrior'.

So, what now? Clearly, I'm battling so much trauma I've put up a wall Trump would be proud of. But I now want that wall to come down. I can only do so if I'm true to myself and ask: what do I actually want?

It's important at this point to say that my experiences aren't the same as every disabled person's out there and I don't want anyone reading this book to not ask out a disabled person for fear they will automatically be seen as a potential devotee or a paedophile. When it comes to dating, my own demons go much deeper than the awful experiences I've had as a disabled woman.

I am also a byproduct of other traumas, like losing my father when I was nine (I always laugh when I say 'losing my father', like I've misplaced him or he's got lost down the frozen pea aisle at Tesco). Losing a parent and, in my case, my only male role model has totally impacted my relationships with men. Call it daddy issues or whatever. In fact, growing up, many of the people I looked up to and admired were all in terrible, toxic relationships. All I saw was pain and heartache. I guess the warrior within, who has protected and served me well growing up 'different', also comes out in full force when dating is concerned.

There will undoubtedly be many disabled people reading this chapter who can 100 per cent relate; others who will sympathise as my fears reflect their own. And still others who are happily in a loving relationship who cannot relate all that much. This is my journey and truthfully, I needed to share it.

I had a very honest and open conversation with my mum about dating during the pandemic when I returned home to shield. She's my best friend and confidante, yet we still, I suppose – as in most parent/child dynamics – aren't so good at talking about sex and relationships. We also never talk about my having children. I can have my own biological children, despite most doctors advising against it, as it would be somewhat complicated and would take careful planning. In other words, pretty much like most things in my life.

During our conversation she said something that broke my heart just a little.

'Samantha, I do worry you are so set in your ways that you won't find anyone and will be alone.'

I guess many parents fear their children won't find a loving partner or will be lonely and that's why I felt a sudden pang of sadness. Not for me, but for her. I never wanted her to worry unnecessarily. I could have taken offence or felt panicked by the comment, yet in that moment I felt resolute. Now, more than ever, my uniqueness was my strength. I've been battling since I was a child to have a normal relationship but I now realised that what I need to do is embrace the fact that the universe has a different path for me.

I would never thrive in a conventional relationship. For starters, I love my space, I love being alone with my thoughts, I hate sharing my bed and love my sleep. I have never needed anyone to complete me; I'm pretty marvellous all by myself. I am exactly where I need to be. I have so much love in my life and I recognise that love comes in all shapes and sizes. I mean my cat Lola is literally my soul mate. She looks at me and there it is, LOVE. She doesn't care if I'm in a wheelchair, if I don't walk, or if I don't brush my hair for days. She just loves me for me. Bruno, on the other hand, only loves me if I have food, so you could say that's just like having a boyfriend?

Sometimes I think I only want to be in a relationship to prove a point when, in fact, I love how fiercely independent I am and how I am pretty darn comfortable in my own company. It's learned behaviour, yes, but that doesn't mean the person I am today is wrong. It's just who I am and for the most part I'm pretty content with how things are.

Plus, studies have shown that living solo means you live longer. Take the Japanese, for example. They have embraced the super-solo society characterised by young people who don't feel the need to get married. Okay, so that's a generalisation, but being comfortable in one's own company is something to truly cherish. It's so important to be in tune with yourself, to be present.

This is exactly what I'm working on, practising mindfulness when it comes to relationships and really listening to my intuition, my gut. I now need to focus not on what I need, but what I want. This is the basis of the law of attraction. Some of my friends have said that I'm just 'not putting myself out there enough' and they are absolutely right. I'm not proactive in any way when it comes to dating. I could do more. I could revisit online platforms. I could set some funds aside that are specifically allocated for the 'disability price tag' extra costs so that I won't feel too hard done by when the date doesn't go my way.

But I have come to the conclusion that I will do all this when I'm ready. I believe I've not invested in dating thus far simply because I don't want it badly enough. And that's okay.

I am still battling my inner demons, which whisper and creep into my mind, telling me that I need to be in a relationship because that is what society dictates. It's most likely the reason I haven't found anyone; because, actually, is it what *I* want right now? Not really. I'm pretty content working on me.

A friend of mine went to a psychic almost eight years ago and, apparently, I popped up in the reading. The psychic told my friend I would only find love in my mid to late thirties. When I heard the news, I was devastated, furious. At the time I was a smoker. I sat, huddled, chain smoking and sobbing, half leaning out of my bedroom window. In tatters. Now, I'm not saying I totally believe my fate was sealed by this psychic, but that prospect no longer terrifies me.

I am now 36 and I truly believe this is the year I will find love. Why? Because I've already been planting the seeds. I agreed to an audition for a well-known celebrity dating television show. Believe me, even a year ago I would have never said yes to a show in which I'd have to be so vulnerable and go on dates with strangers. In the end they didn't cast me for this year's show, but who knows what might happen in the future.

I've also been chatting to a few guys online and have even asked them out for drinks. That hasn't happened yet because of the bloody pandemic, but the conversations have been empowering in many ways. I have controlled the narrative.

I also had a really scary experience not that long back that can only be described as a sexual assault. I considered for a long time whether I wanted to talk about it, and decided it's important and that women shouldn't be afraid to speak of our experiences. What happened to me was not my fault. It wasn't caused by anything I did or said. Sexual violence is never – ever – the fault of the victim, and the only person who bears any responsibility is the perpetrator. In my experience, women are afraid to speak out for two reasons. The first is internalised shame. We ask ourselves, *What could I have done to have made this not happen?* The answer is nothing. Someone decided to commit an act of violence. That was done by them and them alone.

The second reason we fear speaking out is that we may not be believed. This is worse for disabled women. We are infantilised by a society that doesn't like to think of disabled people as sexual beings. We cannot talk about our positive experiences, and we cannot talk about the negative ones either. We somehow find ourselves in a culture that believes that sexual violence is about desirability and, by refusing to see us as fully formed, living adults who experience love and sexual desire, we consign them to the 'undesirable' file. When this happens it's a short step to not believing us when we say we've been assaulted. After all, who would want to assault someone 'undesirable'?

This has to stop. Disabled women are more likely to be the victims of this kind of crime. Often our disability aids are weaponised against us. I was trapped in my wheelchair by my attacker. I've heard stories from other women about prosthetic limbs being taken from them so they cannot defend themselves or their guide dogs being blocked from doing their jobs so the woman could not escape. This has to end. Enough is enough. If we tell you something has happened to us, then believe us.

To be completely honest with you, I'm so tired of burdening myself with the ignorance of others. My life is far too precious to focus any more of my energy on people who cannot see past their own prejudices. The embarrassment I once felt so strongly about being single is slowly dissipating. I shouldn't feel embarrassed by people's inability to see the power and beauty in disability and in me.

So, here's my manifestation . . .

I would love a travel companion, another animal enthusiast who may just be as eccentric as me and want to buy a goat and have an animal sanctuary one day. Someone who loves my scars, my curved spine, my cranky moods when I'm in pain. I want to share my life with someone who feels like they can be their authentic self around me. Someone who farts and leaves the bathroom door open so we can chat. A pasta lover. Someone who isn't scared when I say I don't know what I'm doing and I'm terrified.

I want to be with someone who, like me, is at once fiercely independent and not afraid to ask for help. I also want someone I can create a family with. I'd be a fucking fabulous mother and, if my furless furbabies are anything to go by, any child of mine would never be without love and adoration.

One thing I will never do is change who I am for a partner. I don't need anyone to complete me. I want someone who can be my best mate. If that never happens, I'm cool about it because I have so much richness in my life that I will never be alone.

For anyone in a similar situation, please don't be scared to find joy in your own company. Please don't let society make you feel like an outcast if you don't want to get married, have kids or 'settle down' because, even if we have all these things, it doesn't mean our lives are filled with love and happiness. These qualities start from within. Instead of focusing on who isn't in your life, take a moment to look around and see who is. Even if that is your goldfish called Bert.

I sat in bed the other day, watching television, Lola curled in my lap, feeling her soft purr vibrate against my body. Then Mama Renke broke my concentration.

'Ah, just look at how she's looking at you!'

I glanced down to have my eyes met with the biggest saucers, literally like Puss in Boots from *Shrek*. Lola, one paw on my chest, looking at me, sublimely content. This was unconditional love. I was so grateful. In that moment I honestly felt a sense of calm. I spend so much of my time and energy looking for love when I already have an abundance. I felt a calm because honestly, in that moment, I thought if this is my lot, it's more than I need.

I think we can all be a little guilty of always searching for the next best thing or feeling like we aren't loved when, in fact, we can have all the love we need – if we just work on loving ourselves and take the time to see that love comes in many different shapes and sizes.

9

Reconnecting with Yourself

'Carpe diem.'
(Seize the day)

I 'm writing this final chapter during the week between Christmas and New Year. You know, the one when you literally eat all the remaining chocolate and, if like me you're in a German household, Lebkuchen and Stollen left over from the big day.

It's a time for rest, hangovers, quiet contemplation for the year to come and perhaps the odd panic attack when you realise you will be back at work soon and you've just spent £170 in the Next Boxing Day sale. Gifts you will put away for the following Christmas, thinking you've been savvy and cost effective but in fact you forget where you stashed them so end up buying more anyway.

Nevertheless, you try to put it all to the back of your mind and instead watch endless re-runs on television while telling yourself that showering can wait and that you don't smell like gravy and chipolatas. (You do: I'm a veggie and even I smell of them.)

For me, the best thing about this time of year is cracking open that new diary or journal I got from

Santa and writing out my hopes, dreams and intentions for the year ahead. I wouldn't say they are the same as New Year's resolutions because, let's face it, they are always pretty naff, spun out of capitalist greed and designed to make us feel guilty.

I usually treat myself to a fancy fountain pen for my entries. Why not make everything fabulous? I love doing this because it often calms my anxiety. Writing acts as an anchor, a grounding tool, and it gives me focus and a great sense of calm. I create a world that's safe for me. I am, to an extent, regimented in my planning in my day-to-day life; I need to check venues and transport for their accessibility, and I need to look ahead and work around operations, making my agent, my colleagues and my friends aware of the time I will take to heal.

Yet I also am also mindful of the beauty, serendipity and spontaneity of life. My many broken bones have frequently taken me away from the path I had envisioned and, for many of you reading this book, the global pandemic has also shown that life can change at the drop of a hat and derail our expectations. Nevertheless, this could bring about unforeseen opportunities too and create an openness to new possibilities you never thought imaginable.

I am kind to myself when I write. No pressure or time restrictions. I simply look within and try to envisage what will make me safe, secure and happy for the next 12 months. It's a working document and can be started whenever the heck I want. I dip in and out of it, a lovely reminder of what I am capable of. I'm totally a list maker and list ticker. I just grab those glitter pens and go for it.

I also take this opportunity to practise self-care. I try to avoid any distractions when doing so because I really need to be honest about what I want and what makes me happy without the television blaring, social media giving me FOMO, or naked cats sitting on my head. I just need a good old cup of tea and a copy of *Ideal Home* so I can cut out and stick in beautiful pictures as a reminder that I deserve beautiful things.

It is also an opportunity to work through a lot of my internal anguish or fears. At the moment, I'm facing a few more operations on my legs. I have two non-union fractures in each of my femurs, which basically means both my legs are broken, like all the time, but are held in place with the telescopic rods I had implanted as a child. My bones are desperately trying to knit back together but are doing a piss-poor job so simply aren't healing.

To top it all off, the rods have decided they no longer want to be in my bones after 30 years and have started to migrate, which I find fucking rude as I made them feel totally welcome, but I guess you just can't please everyone. Really not the best timing when you have a book launch you want to savour and enjoy instead of being in some not-so-lovely hospital bed. But this is the beauty of life and its ever-changing nature.

So, I am now making a commitment moving forward to connect to a sense of openness. Openness not to be overwhelmed when my plans are derailed because, if this book has brought about anything within me, it is that I am sure as hell more than capable of coping and flourishing, no matter what.

I've mentioned already my reasoning behind writing this book and wanting to create something in which others can find solace. I've spoken a lot about my disability identity, and I hope that, even if you aren't disabled, you have been able to recognise that we are all humans simply wading our way through this life. Although what I've shared here with you are my stories as a disabled woman, at the core of it all is that each of us strives for and thrives from the same things. We all need love, respect, friendship, success, security and happiness.

I also want you to go away from this book believing that you aren't a problem to be fixed; you aren't wrong. What's wrong is the world we live in, the infrastructure that lets us down. Unburden yourself of this. Be free and unapologetically you.

And remember the following . . .

All bodies are beautiful and sexy

My body is beautiful and sexy; all disabled bodies are beautiful and sexy. We are not ugly or undesirable, we just live in a world where disabled doesn't fit the rigid and unattainable parameters of modern-day beauty standards. Rejection sucks but rejecting yourself sucks even more. Focus on loving yourself.

I really wish we'd talked more about the uniqueness of bodies in school. I wish we'd been taught this when I was a teenager, and we'd learned that disabled people have the same romantic thoughts, sexual desires, lusts and fantasies as anyone else and we should be allowed to explore them.

Don't assume we don't want sex or that we cannot have spontaneous sex or one-night stands. Sure, I've expressed some of the barriers I've faced when dating, but I also want to make it abundantly clear that disabled people should be given a choice when it comes to their sexual interactions.

If you are a parent, I urge you to all buy some dolls with disabilities. I love my wheelchair Barbie. Buy books on neurodivergence and talk about them with your child. Play, be curious and laugh because, honest to the heavens, I don't want the next generation of disabled kids feeling they aren't beautiful, and I don't want anyone to have to go through some of the rather traumatic experiences I've had as a disabled woman simply because we are still too awkward around disability.

I've had some really unpleasant and toxic relationships and sexual experiences because I've not been able to talk and communicate my needs without feeling ashamed or embarrassed. I've learned that communication is key to any relationship, disabled or otherwise. If in doubt, ask.

I've also learned that I feel the sexiest and most confident when I've allowed myself to say no. No, I don't need to have sex when I'm just doing it to simply feel normal. No, my worth is not dependent on how many sexual partners I've had or how regularly I'm doing it. No, I don't have a boyfriend but that's okay and nothing to feel ashamed of because the time I spend not being in a relationship has been quality time in which I've got to know and celebrate who I am as an individual. This I've found to be invaluable.

Boundaries are great but vulnerability is beautiful

Whenever I think of the word 'boundaries', I immediately conjure up an image of me in my wheelchair with cattle prods attached to my wheels so that I can electrocute anyone walking straight towards me as they stare, transfixed, on their mobile phone. If you are this person, please stop, just stop! It's scary and dangerous for many disabled people.

'Boundaries' is a word that gets flung around a lot, but actually figuring out what boundaries are valid and necessary for you and your individual needs is important and doesn't come easily. I've recognised that my internalised ableism makes me feel 'othered', which often leads to a constant need and desire to be liked by everyone. I've been to some amazing events, balls and galas. I've mingled in rooms filled with famous people and, although I've never doubted my worthiness for being invited, I have always left worried, anxious that I've not been liked by everyone I've met. Was I too drunk, too loud, too opinionated? The fact is, we can't be liked by everyone and to try to be invariably means our boundaries get blurred; you can't please all the people all the time and frankly, what other people think of us is none of our business.

I've also learned that it's okay to call out ableism and ableist microaggressions. You are not being 'woke' when doing so. For years, I would never say boo to a goose. I wanted to be liked; I never wanted to rock the boat. But years of negative, discriminatory and ableist interactions knocked my sense of worth. I allowed myself to become my label. I became infantile, not raising my voice. I chose pleasing others over pleasing myself. Now I leave behind the urge to put other people's comfort before my own discomfort. It's okay to call out any shitty and ignorant behaviour. Being told you are being overly sensitive, politically correct or woke is just another form of control and oppression.

You don't always have to be strong; asking for help is the bravest thing you can ever do. One of the qualities I am most grateful for as a result of being born with a disability is the ability to ask for help, whether that be asking someone in a shop to grab me some milk from a top shelf or asking other disabled people for advice on how to claim a benefit that helps me go to work. I think we are programmed to view asking for help as a sign of weakness because being vocal about one's needs shines a big old bright light on how difficult and challenging life can be. But if we never ask for help it stops us from calling out or identifying all the barriers and hardships we have to deal with daily. It stops us speaking our mind, it stops us from sharing our commonalities and lived experiences. It stops us from saying that life is hard.

I know many of my peers find it hard to accept help from non-disabled people and many of my non-disabled friends struggle over whether or not they should offer help to someone disabled. I get it: you don't want people to assume you can't because of your disability and many disabled people really don't need assistance. I'm a total pampered poodle and if I can delegate to others, that's fine with me. But the bottom line is that showing vulnerability, offering or receiving help has led to some of the most humbling and real interactions I've had in my life. For me, it's not about being patronising, it's not about making assumptions or having people judge your capabilities. It's about two humans interacting and showing kindness. You can disagree with me, but I think we could all do with a bit more kindness in our lives.

Disabled people are pretty fucking amazing

I still can't believe I went most of my life without embracing other disabled people. We've established this wasn't my fault or the result of being a bad person, but rather my internalised ableism at work. Also, it's important to note that disabled people aren't all the same. Some are wonderful, others proper wankers.

We don't just all live harmoniously simply because of the commonality of our disabilities. In fact, I don't look at another wheelchair user or person with brittle bones and want to become their BFF and I find it patronising when I am pushed to befriend someone with a disability, like we all need to keep to our own. But I can categorically say that my life is richer and fuller now I have a diverse group of friends and colleagues.

I've been invited to a number of social engagements recently where a mutual friend has introduced me to a group of already well-established cliques. To be honest, I love these kinds of engagements because I love people. But on each occasion, I noticed something. I was never asked a question. No one interacted with me unless I offered up information or my mutual friend included me in the conversation, as a third party. It struck me that we are conditioned to stick to what or who we know.

By contrast, I seek new adventures, opportunities and people. I thrive off them and I appreciate I'm incredibly privileged to have this confidence. But I've also learned to be this way. Perhaps that person you dismissed or were awkward or shy around could have had the potential to have been your new best friend, lover, start-up partner, inspiration or fellow *Buffy the Vampire Slayer* enthusiast who will never judge you for your love of naked cats.

I don't want to shame anyone who finds social interactions like these overwhelming, or those of you who are introverts. I am simply saying that we should try to find a way that feels safe and comfortable to get to know those you may have overlooked in the past. Be a little bit more curious, seek the beauty in others and don't be afraid to be vulnerable.

Each of you has something valuable to contribute. A story to share and wisdom to impart. But we will only know the wonders each of us possess if we set aside our own insecurities, prejudices and unconscious biases. Next time you are out and about, try to have a spontaneous connection, start a dialogue with a person you don't know and smile at a stranger.

Find what makes you happy

I want everyone to find their happiness, but also to recognise that happiness is like the seasons – always in constant flux. Always evolving, growing as we grow. Changing as we change.

I've shared with you my most intimate life journeys. My path to success and my moments of complete triumph. But as I sit here and reflect on most of my life, I have to acknowledge that I have often been living for the benefit and happiness of others, rather than for myself. A lot of my time and energy has been spent either trying to prove I am 'normal' and capable, or that disability isn't a dirty word.

I think I've pretty much nailed the message. I know I have because I often get the awkward, ableist backhanded compliment that 'you aren't like other disabled people!', as though we are all supposed to live up to the same stereotype.

I don't regret living my life in this way and I've undoubtably profited and prospered from pushing the parameters of societal norms and barriers. But I'm tired. I think that's the best way to describe how and where I am in my life. I'm tired of being an extravagant, larger-than-life version of who I am. I say 'larger-than-life' as I don't believe I'm living a falsehood, more a version of Samantha who is always on her A-game.

I love that Samantha – she is a badass bitch – but I need now to only bring her out when it really counts because sometimes that Samantha loses sight of what I truly want and what makes me authentically happy. I need to be more vulnerable and let people see the other sides of me. The times I can't get out of bed or when I am physically sick with worry. The times when actually

I don't want to be around anyone and when I am experiencing campaigning fatigue. The times when I don't know what to say or haven't yet come to an opinion on something. Or the times when I really fuck up. I want to be able to put my hands up and say I don't always get it right.

I'm learning each day that happiness is amplified the more we are grateful. No matter who we are, what our circumstances are, we can find things to be grateful for.

This was true for me during the pandemic, for many of us one of the toughest challenges we've had to face. The uncertainty, instability and fear left us all feeling defenceless. For many, this was combined with the realisation that others around us did not share the same views as us and now our eyes are open to a new harshness in society, and that is scary. As someone who was once again given the label 'vulnerable', I was faced with my life changing dramatically.

I felt loneliness like never before. I felt impermanence as a disabled person, especially given that one in six deaths came from the disability community. I also found it hard to find empathy for those who struggled with lockdown, knowing that a disabling world will live on after any pandemic and that for many disabled people, lockdown is 365 days a year.

Yet I took full advantage of the new way of working. My anxiety flares up when I have to travel by unreliable and inaccessible public transport, or I attend meetings in buildings that are not wheelchair 'friendly'. The words 'we'll just carry you up to the third floor' fill me with dread. All of these barriers were removed during the pandemic and my business flourished as everything was brought online. My mental health improved, too, as I was no longer paralysed by the prospect of many of the barriers I'm used to.

Of course, there is always a balance to be struck. I experienced loneliness and became complacent in some areas. I didn't take as many risks as before or say yes to as many opportunities. But what this time did was highlight the fact that doing more of the things I feel happiest doing gives me an enormous amount of peace.

Moving forward, it has allowed me to show the world that we don't have to be as we once were and that's okay. It also gave me reassurance that, even when the whole world came to a standstill, I didn't.

I moved to London many years ago because it's the 'place to be' – I believed you have to be in the heart of it to be successful. You have to sacrifice things to get what you want. I've now realised this is utter bollocks. Yes, resources and opportunities are disproportionately still centred around capital cities. Prejudices towards small-town folk do exist and there is still a pressure to be a team player and a part of every event. FOMO is alive and well. But I've come to the conclusion that only *you* bring happiness to you, not anyone else.

Moving to London was one of the best moves I've ever made. But I've now let go of any fear that my success and happiness can only come from living there. Fear that for many years kept me in London, in a small flat with windows I couldn't see out of, with lifts that broke and venues that I could not access. Fear that if I left, my success would be over too. What I crave now are the sounds of birds and being closer to family.

Now that fear has lifted and, you know, even if for whatever reason my work dries up, I know that I have the strength to succeed in anything else I put my mind to. Because I am the person I've invested in, love and believe in.

If you want something, go for it

I don't often say this, aloud or to anyone really, but the truth is I really want to become a mother. I don't know why this should be such a revelation; many people become parents, and no one bats an eyelid. For me, I have never been asked if I want to be a mother. Some assume I can't have children and others assume I simply wouldn't want to. Some worry how I'd cope, as though having a disability would make parenthood unbelievably difficult, so why would I burden myself? Some worry about the children themselves, as though they'd suffer from having a disabled parent. For me this seems like the biggest taboo and something I've thought about since I was a very young child.

People become parents for a whole host of reasons, and I guess I'm no different. Maybe we want that unconditional love. Or maybe we want kids to bring purpose to our lives. We might even start a family because our religion dictates it, or because we feel societal pressures to do what is the norm. In all honesty, one of the main reasons I got my Lola was because I wanted to see how I'd cope with the responsibility of another life. I wanted to see how I'd navigate cleaning out her litter tray even though I can't reach down to it. How I'd feed her if I couldn't place her bowl on the ground or how I'd get her to the vet in an emergency.

I appreciate children are a totally different ballgame, but you see where I am going with this. I had once again allowed those ableist thoughts to impinge on my sense of worth. This time it is different. This time I am not trying to prove anything to the outside world. I look back on my life and, literally from the moment I could start to understand the world around me, I've been battling to prove people wrong. My whole life, my career and my strength to succeed in all that I do have been driven by ignorance from those around me.

Motherhood is different and that's why it scares me the most. I have always wanted to be a mother because, above all, I think I will be goddamn amazing at it. I know I will be the best mum in the world. I have so much love to give and I know that like everything else in my life I will exceed expectations. My parenting may not be conventional – I will absolutely have to think outside of the box as I navigate my day-to-day challenges – but unconventional doesn't mean wrong or unworthy of existing.

When has my different outlook ever been detrimental? My uniqueness has been my strength and that is why I will be an amazing parent. And yet, not having that drive behind me, the one that pushes me to do things to prove a point, is the one thing stopping me moving forward. I need to start living life for me and not for others and that's terrifying on every level.

I need to take my own advice and reach out to the wonderful disability community because they will be my point of reference, a wealth of wisdom and a collective ear to listen. I also need to vocalise my wants to those who are closest to me because right now I'm stuck in violin mode. I'm angry and sad that I'm not seen as a possible mother and that no one is asking me if they can help on this journey.

I'm the one who needs to break the silence. Listen, I want to become a mother, so please support me and help me find out what my options are. Fostering, adoption, natural birth, freezing my eggs, IVF? Whatever my journey looks like, I don't want to be on my own. I don't need judgement, comparison, your own fears or prejudice projected onto me. I just want love, respect and support in my choice. This is me asking for help and being totally vulnerable. If you can support me, offer advice and help me on my journey to motherhood I am open and ready to receive.

I wanted to end with one of the most beautiful and powerful lessons I've been given. In fact, my biggest gift came from my greatest loss. It is that we should all seize the moment because life is short. Precious. We navigate this world blissfully floating from one moment to another. Second, minute, hour, day, month, year . . . yet we rarely stop and take time to think about how fleeting our time here truly is. When perhaps we should. Not in a morbid, apocalyptic, we're-all-going-to-die way, but so that we see the beauty in our fragility.

I dedicated this book to my dad, Carl Thomas Renke, who passed away in 1996 when he was just 38 years old. I am now 36 and that, in itself, is rather heart-breaking to me. I feel like my life is just getting good, getting going.

I know that my dad always struggled with my dis-ability. He held on to a guilt as though, somehow, he'd made this broken child and could have done something to have prevented it. He subscribed to the narrative that disability was a tragedy and only saw a life for me that had been dictated by the outside world. He left this earth not seeing how amazingly happy and thriving I am. Yet in the same breath he was my biggest cham-pion. His life was certainly not in vain, and I truly live in his honour.

I awoke to a noise one November morning, a sound similar to that of snoring. Aged only nine, I thought nothing of it, simply drifting in and out of sleep in my princess four-poster bed. My dad had made it as I couldn't be in an average-sized bed for fear I'd fall out and break every bone in my body and by this point I was too old for a cot. He had fashioned a wooden frame around a single mattress on the floor, so I could bum shuffle in and out independently. He used staircase spindles as the four posts and my mum had sewn bespoke curtains and a canopy to complete the effect. The walls were a candyfloss-pink stripe at the bottom, with a dado rail separating it from the blue paper above with its white fluffy clouds. A dreamy, happy room for a happy child, strewn with Troll dolls and Sylvanian Families figures.

It was an unusually bright day for mid-November, but the harshness of the light didn't deter me from falling back to sleep as I waited for Mama Renke to get me up for school. As she gently rocked me to wake up, the noise was still there. I made her aware of it and we almost had a giggle about it as we thought Dad was playing a trick.

She went to investigate. He wasn't in the bedroom as she'd originally thought, so she turned next door towards the bathroom. On opening the bathroom door, she saw my father slumped, his body limp on the floor. He lay between the landing and bathroom. Even as a nurse, my mum was in shock and struggled to remain composed. She put him into the recovery position. We only had one telephone upstairs, situated in my parents' room. I had to crawl over my father to call for the ambulance.

Stephanie didn't hear our cries for help as she was drying her hair downstairs. Our Labrador began to bark to try to alert her, but it felt like hours before she came upstairs. I remember dialling 999, but the first time nothing happened, no dial tone, nothing. Eventually I got through and tried to remember my address. I heard a woman's voice telling me to get my sister from downstairs. When I replied that I couldn't walk, she told me I was in shock.

I was crying at this point, not wanting to look back into the hallway. 'I can't,' I replied, over and over again, eventually yelling, 'I can't walk because I'm disabled!'

Before I knew it, Stephanie had grabbed the phone away from me.

The paramedics strapped my dad to a chair and carried him outside. As we left to follow, my mother carrying me, I looked across the road and my eyes met those of my best friend, Laura. We were supposed to be picking her up to walk to school together. I could see Laura and her mum's relief when they realised I wasn't the one who needed the ambulance. I've never wished I could walk but, in that moment, I wished I'd been able to run over to Laura and never let her go.

You know it's bad news when the doctors usher you into the family room. The emergency team were trying to save my dad. I remember seeing a scan of his brain, the largest dark shadow covering a third of it. I'd already been around hospitals far too much at this point so I knew that this was really bad.

We kept Dad on life support for 48 hours and, although he looked like he was sleeping, he was clinically dead. The haemorrhage had swamped his brain, like a tsunami washing away a whole village. I lay on the bed next to him, Mum and Steph by his side as we said goodbye.

I was already a very anxious child, and this trauma was almost too much for my tiny body to cope with. I had been constantly vomiting and hadn't held anything down since my dad had been taken in, so later that day I went to the tuck shop with my uncle to get some chocolates. On the way back to the ward, I saw the mother of one of my classmates waiting by the reception. I'm still not sure why she was there, but she stopped me and asked if I was okay. I looked at her and simply said: 'No, my dad's dead!'

I am sharing this with you all because, in that moment, my life altered forever. Before my dad died, we had put our home up for sale, Mama Renke had started to retake her nursing qualifications and we had applied for a visa to move to New Zealand. We had family there and wanted a new start. My dad didn't want me to go to high school – he was so fearful of what that looked like for me – and had already made plans for home schooling. We'd buy a large campervan and even explore America too.

It's a lot to get your head around, knowing how unbelievably different your life would have been and how everything changes in an instant. I now never allow myself to go down the what-if rabbit hole. I don't think that's healthy. Instead, I take away the hardest life lesson and I am grateful for it.

People assume my disability is the reason for my motivation, my driving force, the source of all my determination and positive outlook on life. The inspiration porn we all crave: the uplifting story of triumph over adversity. True, my uniqueness has been a blessing not a curse and my desire to prove people wrong has been the biggest metaphorical hot poker up my bum I could ever want in terms of giving me motivation, but the loss of my father is the main reason I am as strong as I am today.

It's hard, and it certainly doesn't make light of my grief. I would give anything to have him here today. I mourn each day that he isn't here and I bitterly regret that he had such a short time on this earth. I still get angry that he had to sacrifice so much. But his sacrifice only makes it easier for me to keep soaring.

I am grateful because his death has made me fight for life. Every operation, every opportunity that terrifies me and every moment where I think I simply can't go on, I stay strong because my dad's death gave me the gift of mindfulness. It reminds me every day that all we have is now. *Carpe diem.*

For many of us, contemplating the finality of life is terrifying, anxiety-inducing. But being faced with death, as I was, or even simply being mindful of it, can actually wake us up. If we accept the ephemeral nature of all our lives, we can actually become more motivated. More present in each and every moment. I didn't come to this conclusion overnight. I felt anger, sadness and fear for many years that followed. Yet, as I grew, I saw that my greatest loss was my biggest reason to live. He lives on in me, in my blood and my heart and mind.

There truly is no right or wrong way to be. Embrace all aspects of yourself. Celebrate your uniqueness. Remember you are not alone. Talk more, with others and yourself, even though it may often feel like you are battling the entire world, taking on everyone's opinions, judgements and preconceived ideas of what makes a human. Which lives have more worth, value or happiness.

Next time someone has an opinion on how you should be, simply reply, 'If you want my life, you can pay my bills too.' But if witty, snide comebacks aren't your forté, then take comfort in the fact you recognise the worth within, and you are doing things that make you truly happy.

I made the silly error during the writing of this book of taking a look at reviews of a few well-known books already published. I sat in horror, scrolling through the harsh and personal attacks some people had left online, and it sent me into a total anxiety spin. The comments weren't about me, of course, but I'd already formulated in my mind the comments that people would make about my book.

I really had to calm myself down. I took some deep breaths and I practised what I preach. *All we have is now.* I asked myself: am I proud of this book? Answer: hell yes. Well then, that's all that matters.

And I am proud. I knew this day would come as a youngster and I made it happen. If this book is well received, that's a bonus. If it helps others, that's a bigger bonus. But my happiness is bound only in how I see my own worth.

So, surround yourself with whatever brings you joy and never let anyone else dictate to you what life you lead. I am grateful for who I am and for every experience I've had and am yet to have because it's my unique life.

So, say it with me now . . .

I am the best thing since sliced bread.

Acknowledgements

To my father, Carl Thomas Renke

You left this earth far too soon and you didn't get to see how I turned out. Well, Dad, I'm bloody wonderful – amazing, in fact – and I'm part of you. You carried the world on your shoulders and I know you worried about me but I just want to say that there was no need because I'm living a vibrant life. I am not just surviving, I'm thriving. I'm happy and I'm very loved. Everything I do is in your honour and this book, my success and happiness is for you. Love you, Dad. You gave me the greatest life lesson: life is short, so live it.

My sister 'Steffi'

I feel like this book should have been called 'life lessons from a sister' because your advice and guidance has been integral to my strength. You challenge me like no one else ever dares. You've always had my back and you've always pushed me when I felt like giving up. They say you can choose your friends but you can't choose your family – well, we would probably both agree that there were many years that we wouldn't have chosen each other as sisters, but even then you believed in me and you bloody pushed me to believe in myself. I am so blessed to say that now I would pick you above anyone else. You are my number-one cheerleader.

Ina, aka Mama Renke

I opened up my heart and soul in this book and expressed my wants and desires like never before. I bared all because I want to start my own family, because I want to have the love you have for me. A mother's love is like no other and I'm grateful to have that love in my life. You are my best friend.

Boy George

Our self-belief should come from within, but it doesn't do us any harm when we get a little reminder from others about our worth. So, you can only imagine how much joy I had when none other than Boy George himself went on live television and said that, in his eyes, I was indeed the best thing since sliced bread. I may have recorded that interview and played it over and over during the months I spent writing this just to remind myself of this fact. Thank you for being a fan; feel free to say more nice things about me.

Acknowledgements

Fearne Cotton

When Fearne Cotton asks you to write a book you say an almighty 'YAS Queen!' Then you rush to the toilet and follow this up by sending Fearne a WhatsApp voicenote telling her that she gave you anxiety poos.

Fearne, you are one special human. You have shown me like no other how to see the sparkle in others. You've allowed me to shine and I'm forever grateful. My fellow cat lady, I'm so blessed to call you my mate.

Lola and Bruno

I love how you both remind me that unique is beautiful and you've shown me what unconditional love is even when you poop outside your litter box. Also, you are both fast on your way to celebrity status; I think I see a children's book in the future called *Lola and Bruno's Naked Adventures . . .*

Buffy the Vampire Slayer

You taught me to slay every day, and that's exactly what I'm doing!